Midnight Edition

Ugh, I Can't EVEN

A SNARKY MANDALA COLORING BOOK: MANDALAS? MEH.

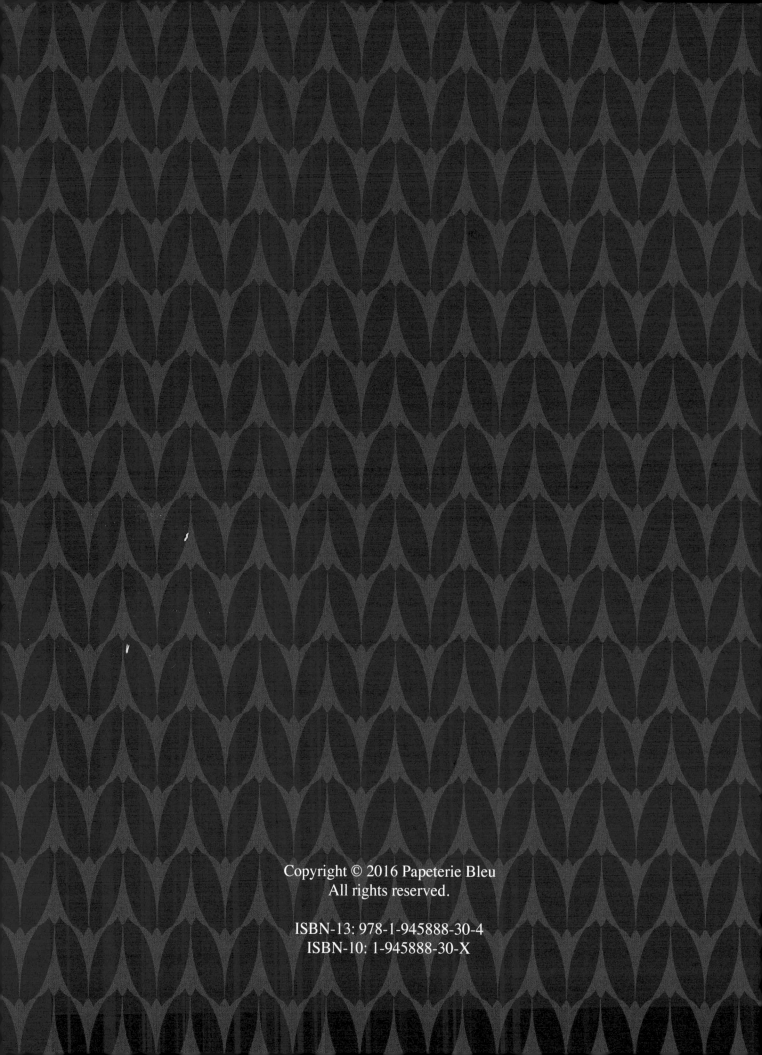

ISBN-13: 978-1-945888-30-4
ISBN-10: 1-945888-30-X

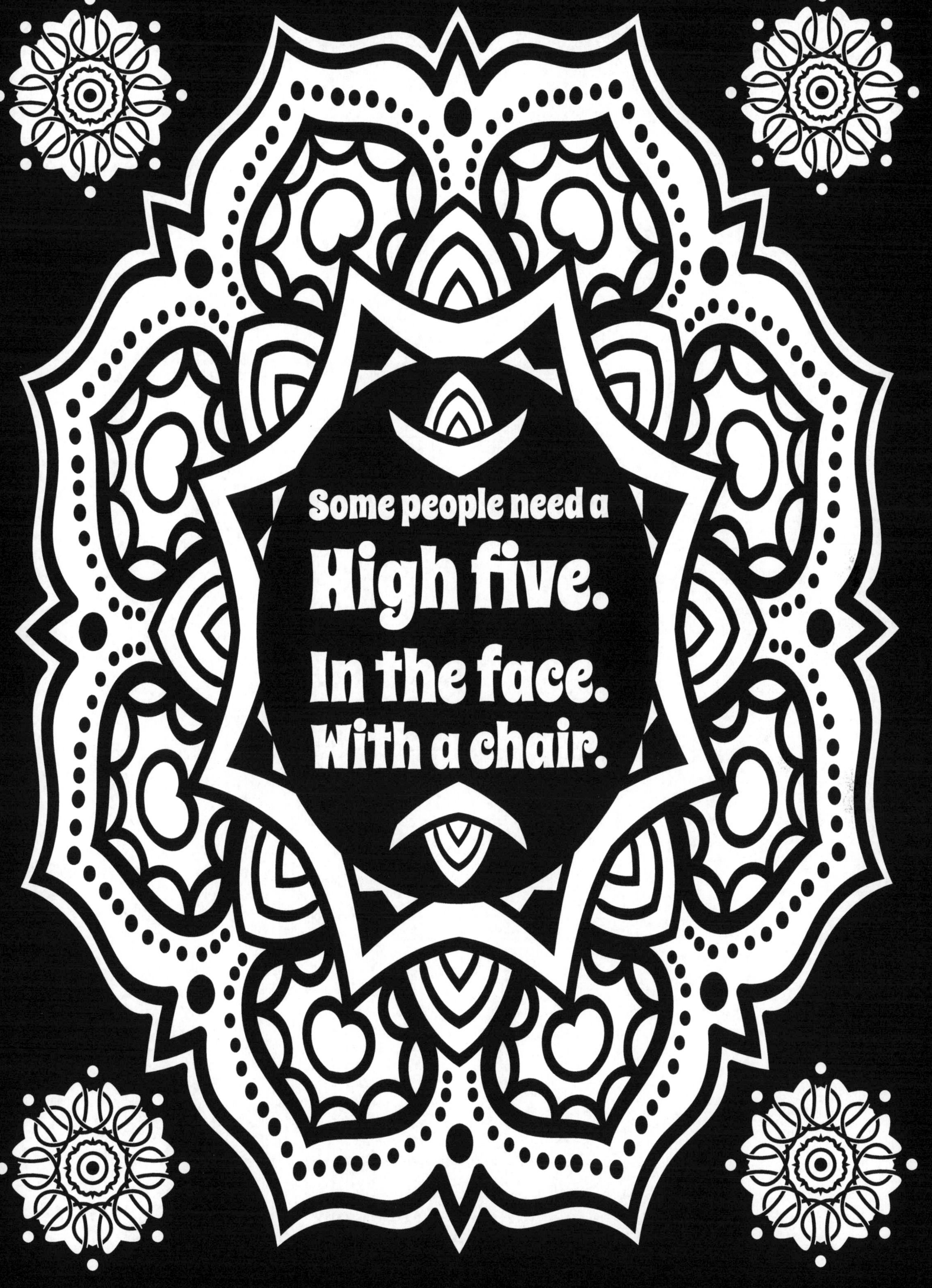
Some people need a
High five.
In the face.
With a chair.

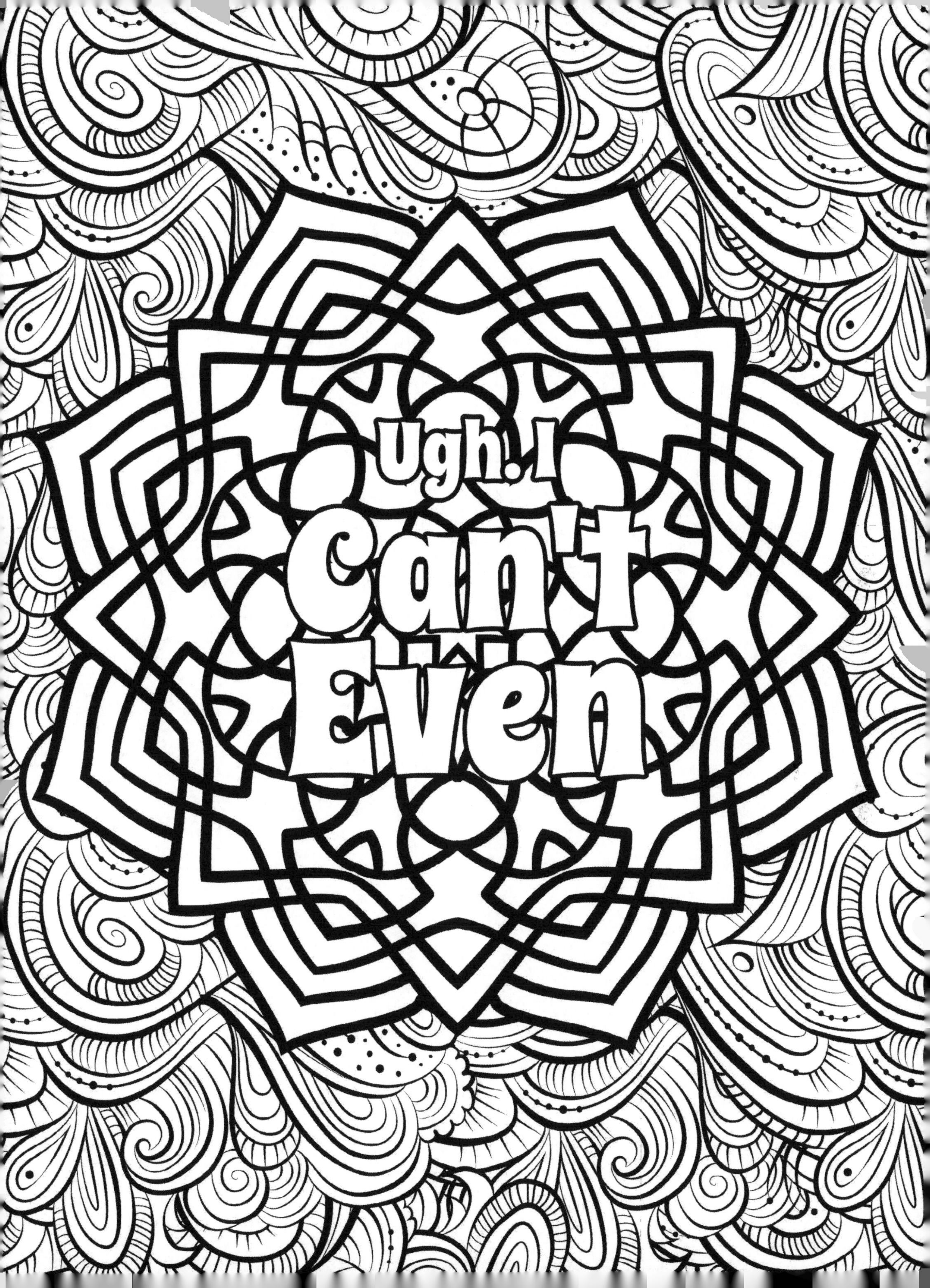
Ugh. I
Can't
Even

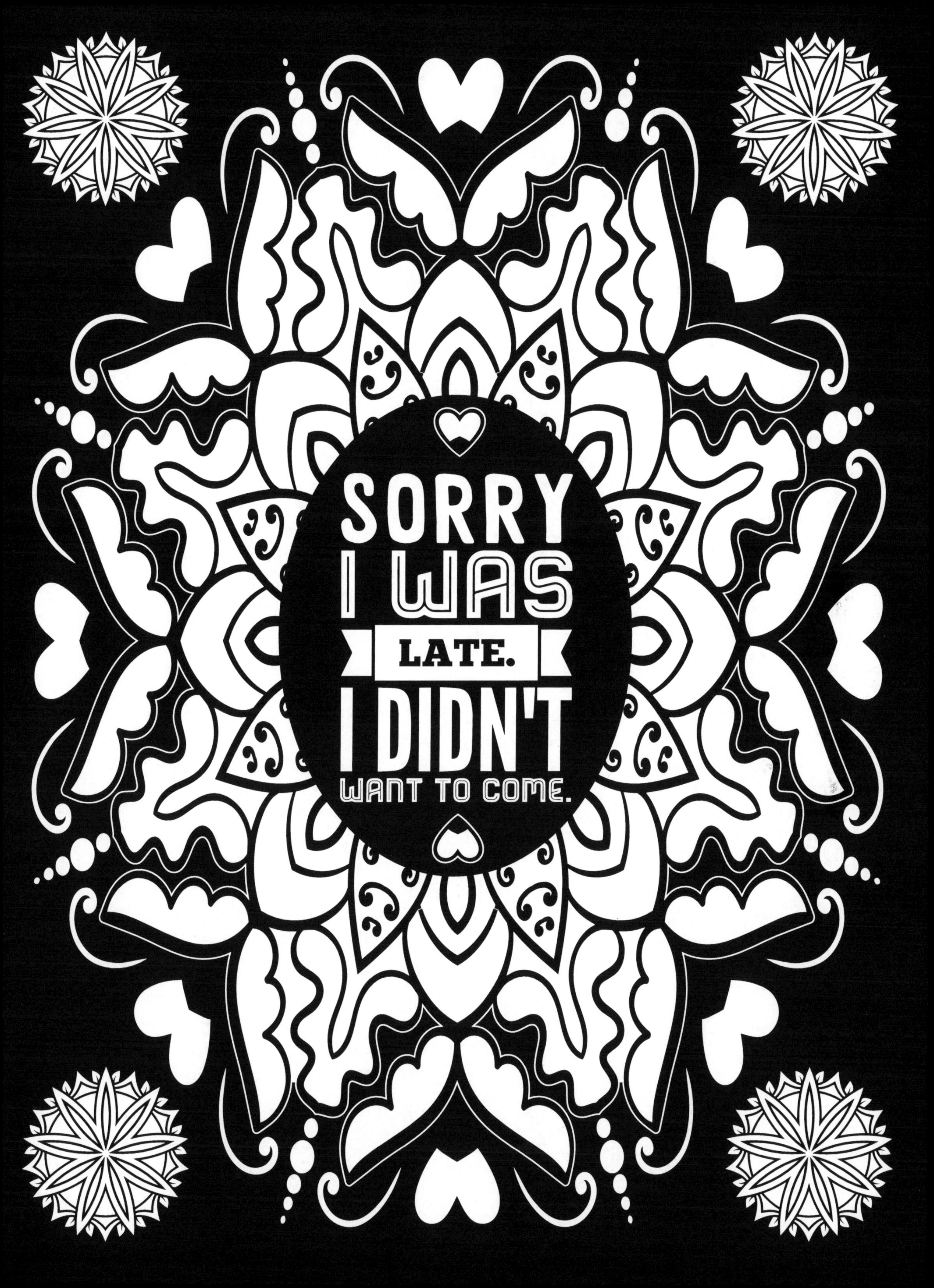
SORRY
I WAS
LATE.
I DIDN'T
WANT TO COME.

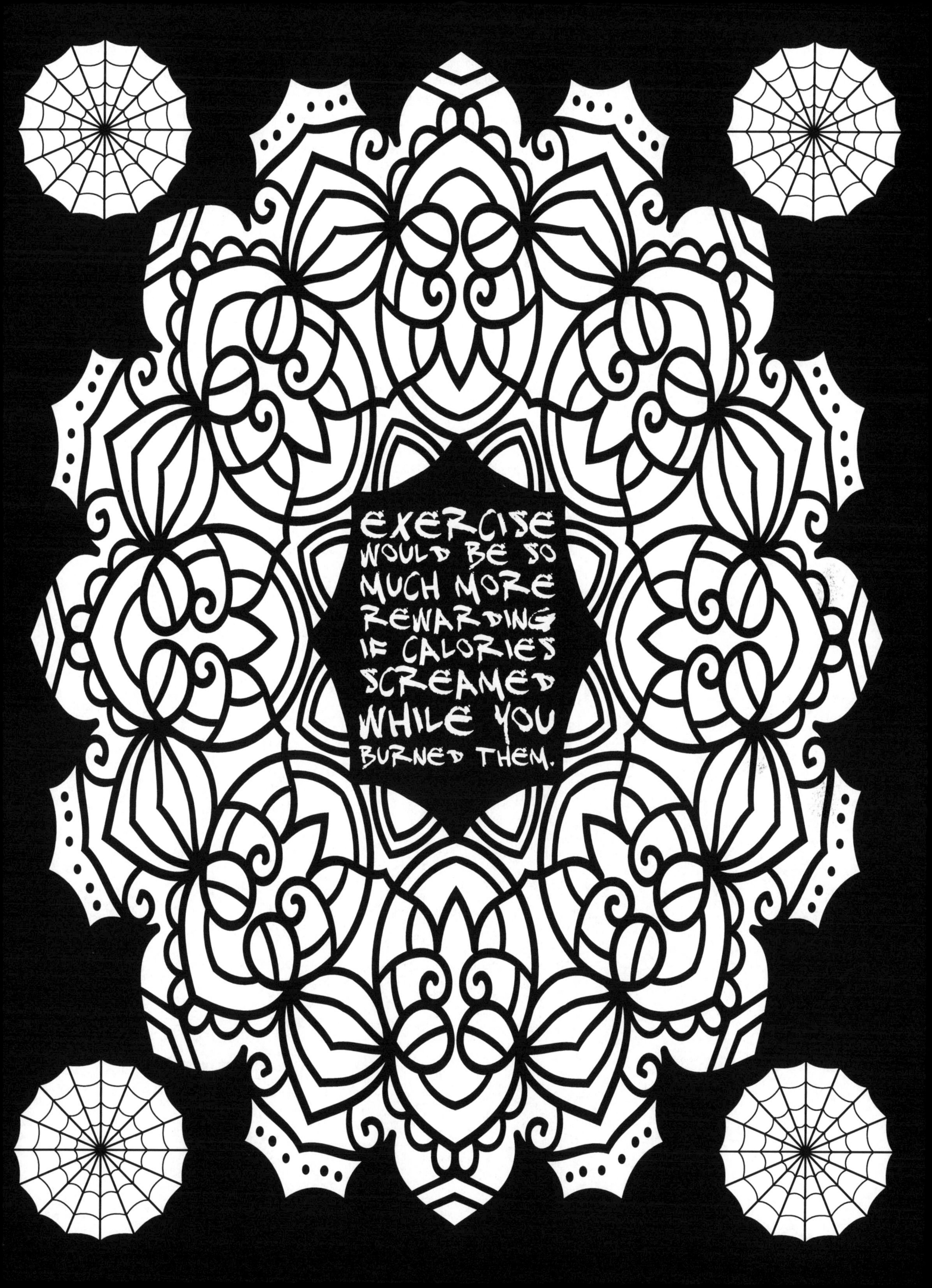
EXERCISE WOULD BE SO MUCH MORE REWARDING IF CALORIES SCREAMED WHILE YOU BURNED THEM.

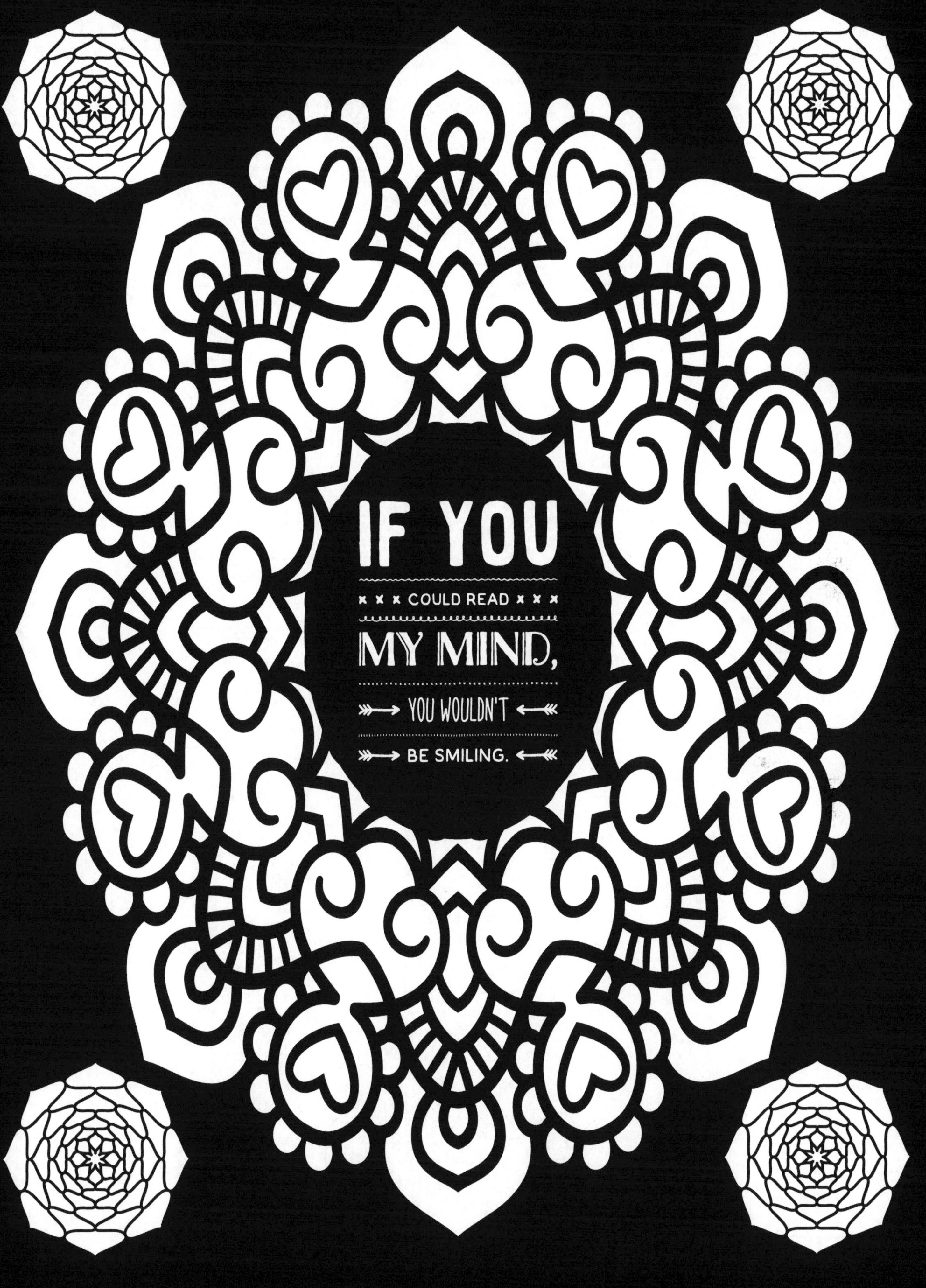
IF YOU
COULD READ
MY MIND,
YOU WOULDN'T
BE SMILING.

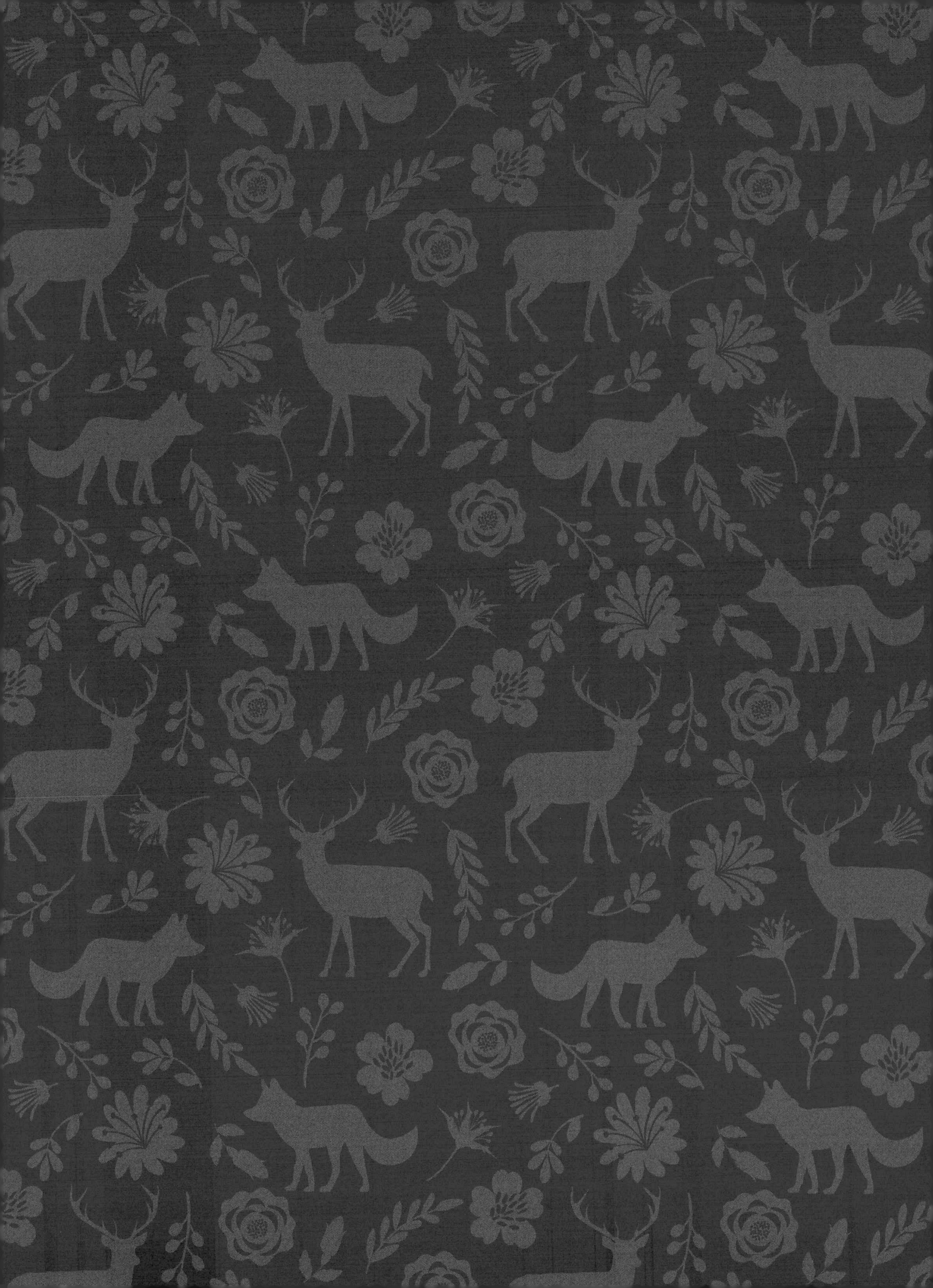

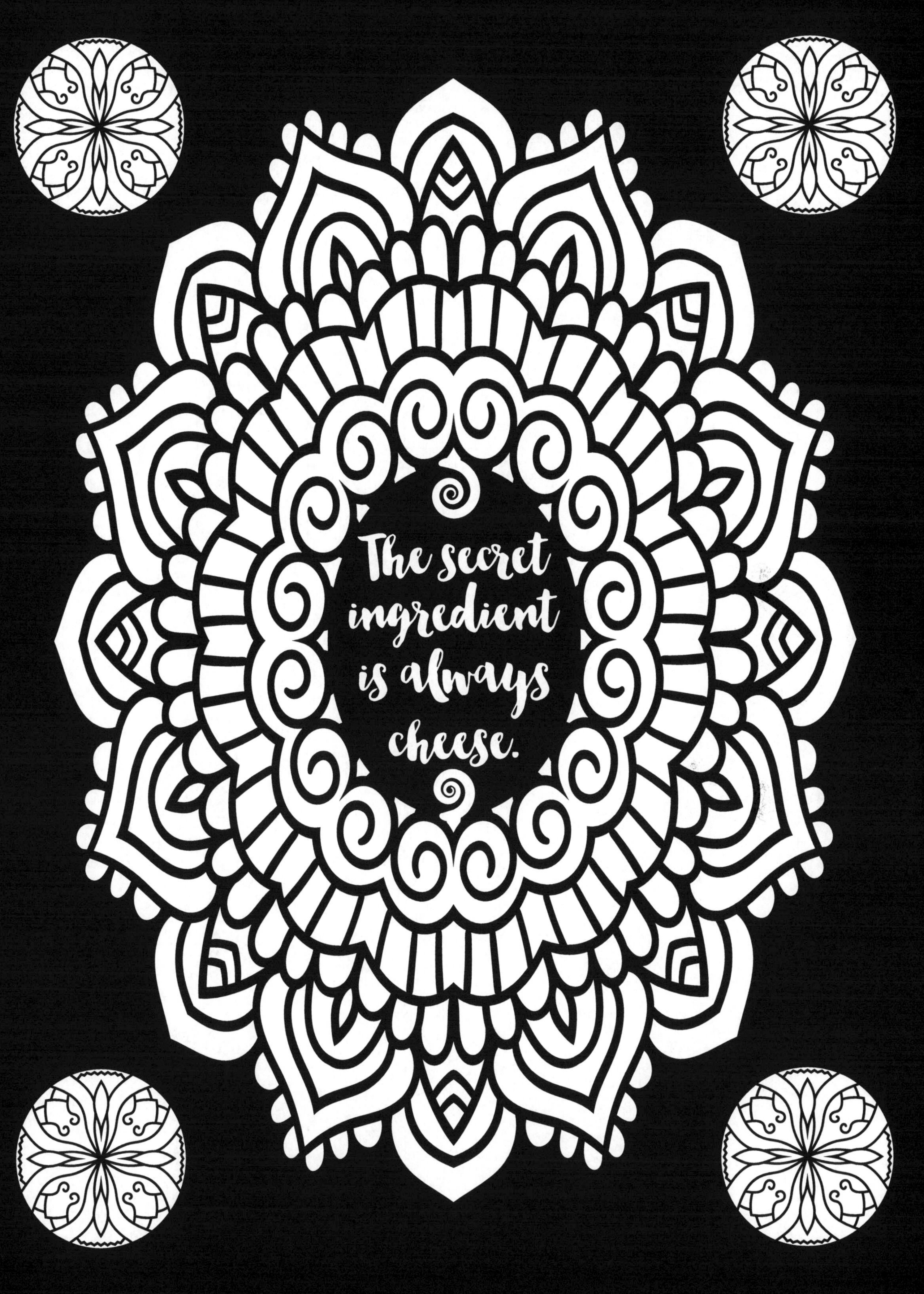
The secret
ingredient
is always
cheese.

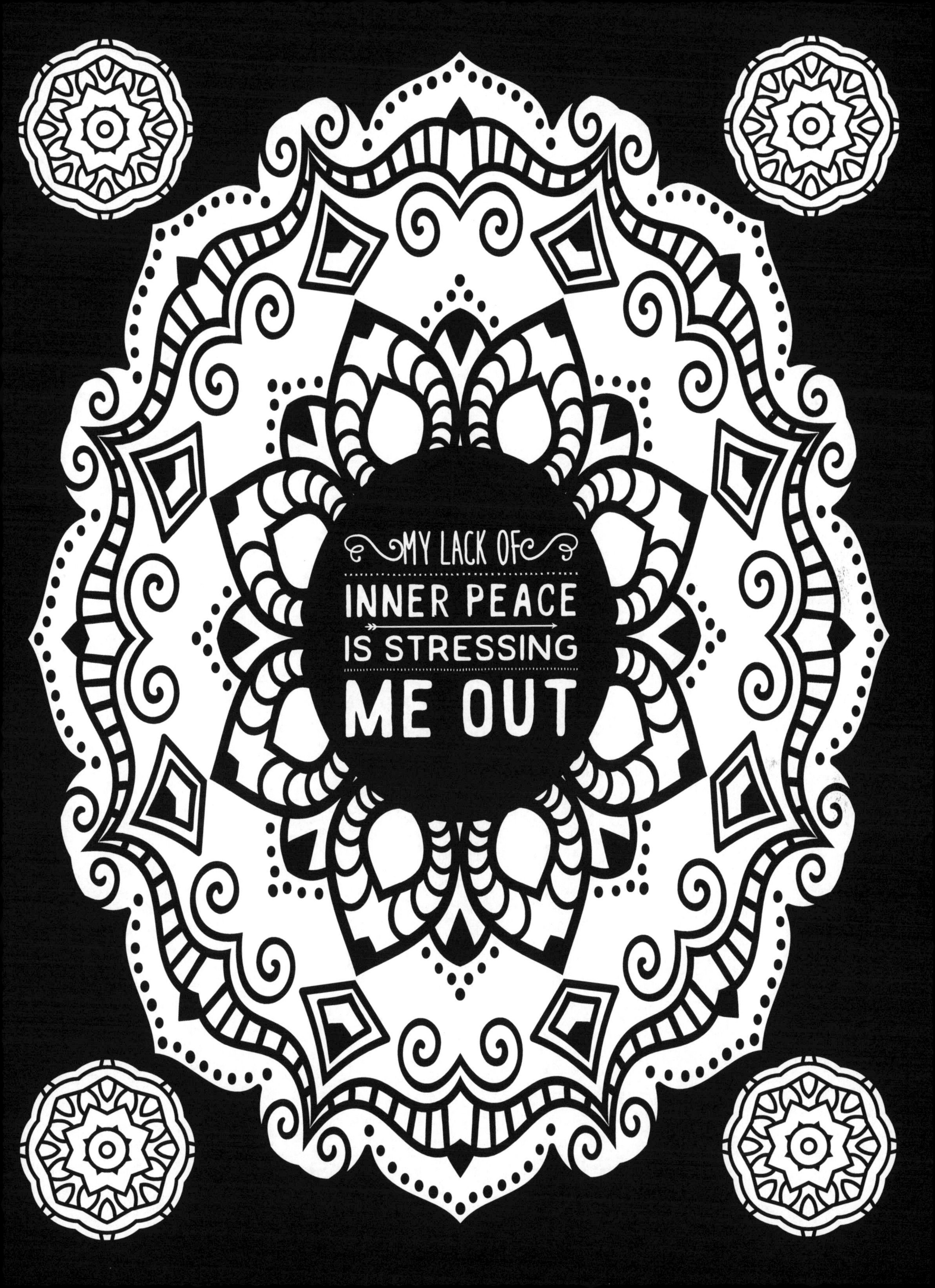
MY LACK OF
INNER PEACE
IS STRESSING
ME OUT

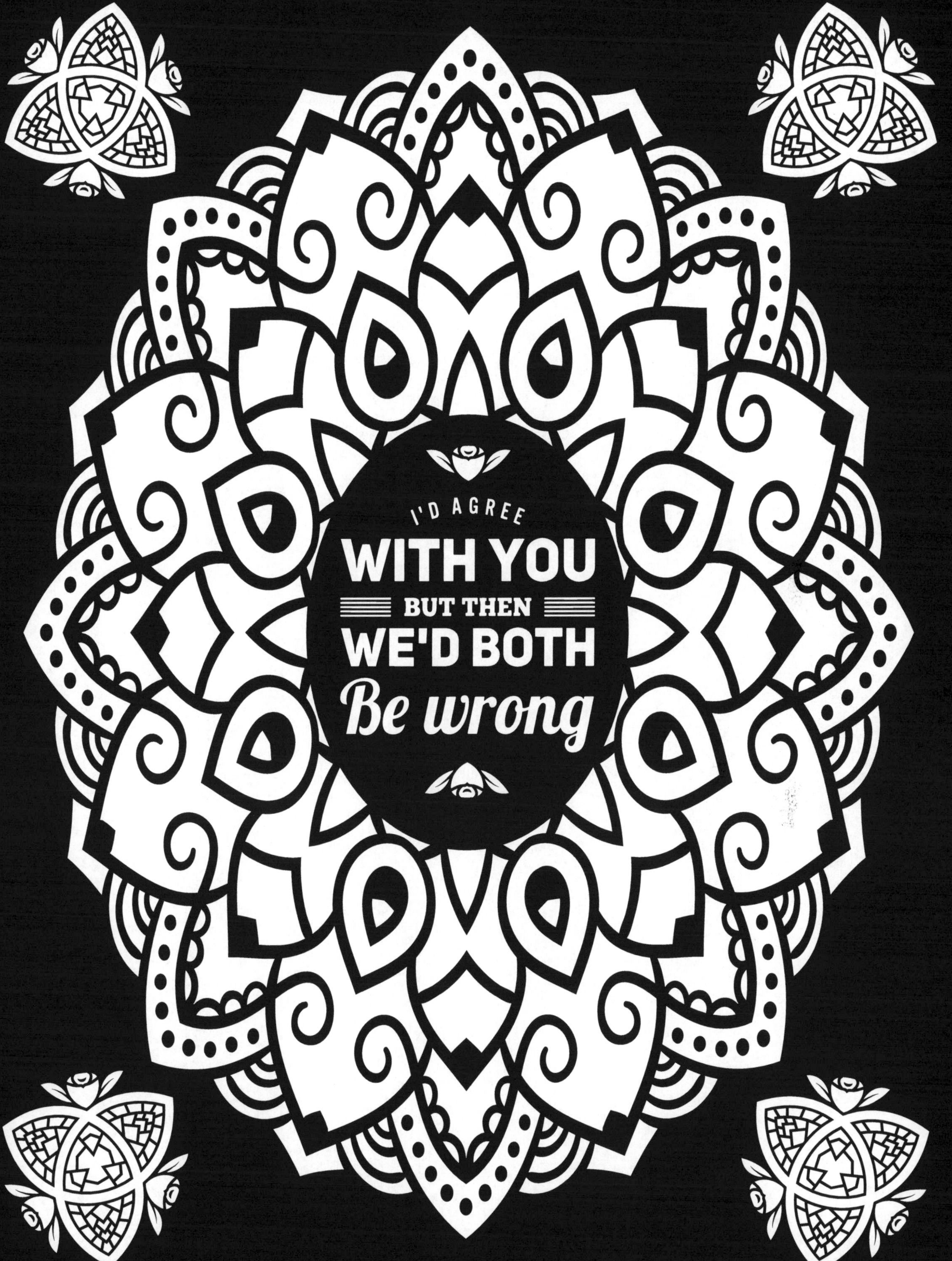
I'D AGREE
WITH YOU
BUT THEN
WE'D BOTH
Be wrong

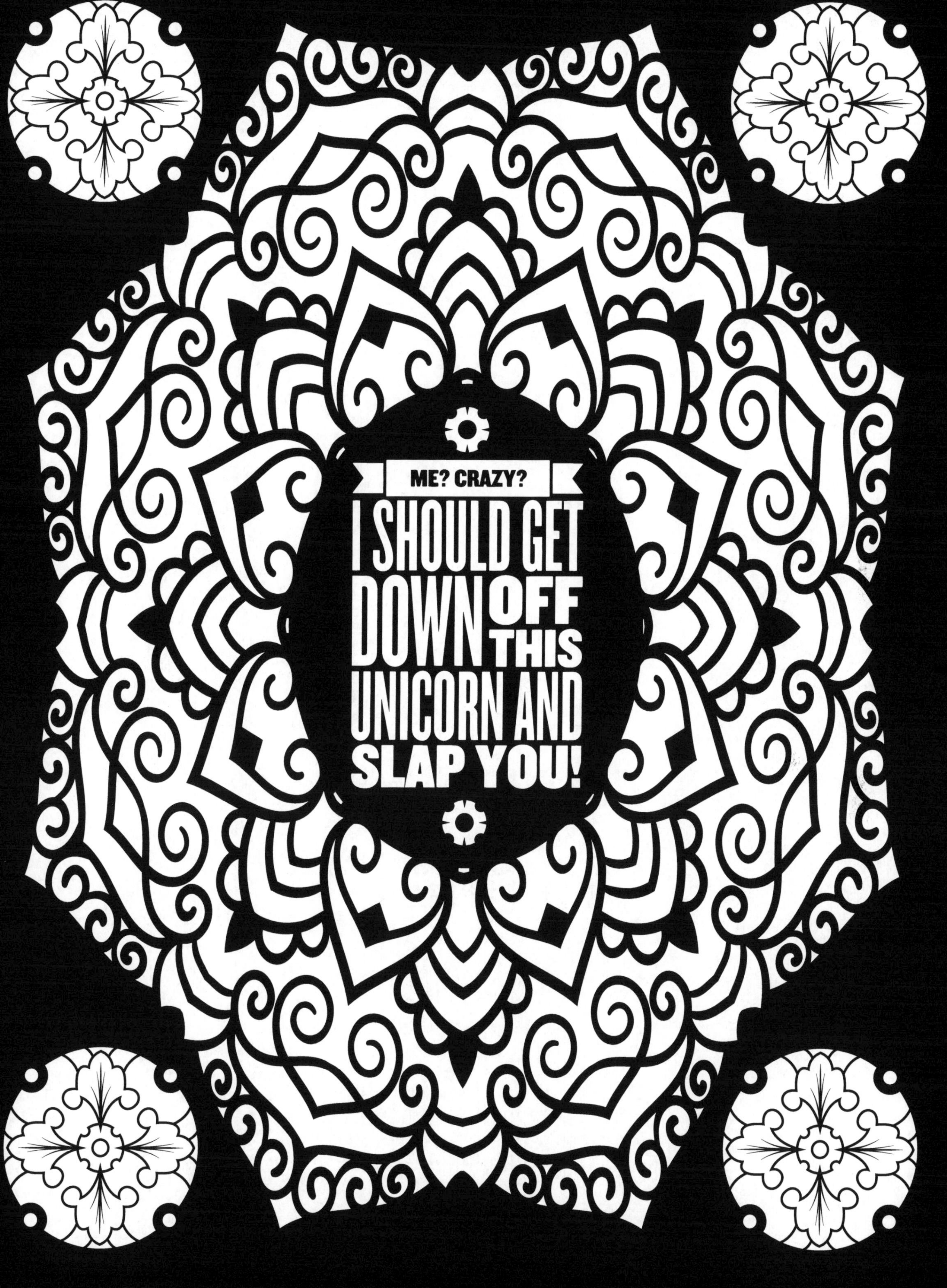
ME? CRAZY?
I SHOULD GET DOWN OFF THIS UNICORN AND SLAP YOU!

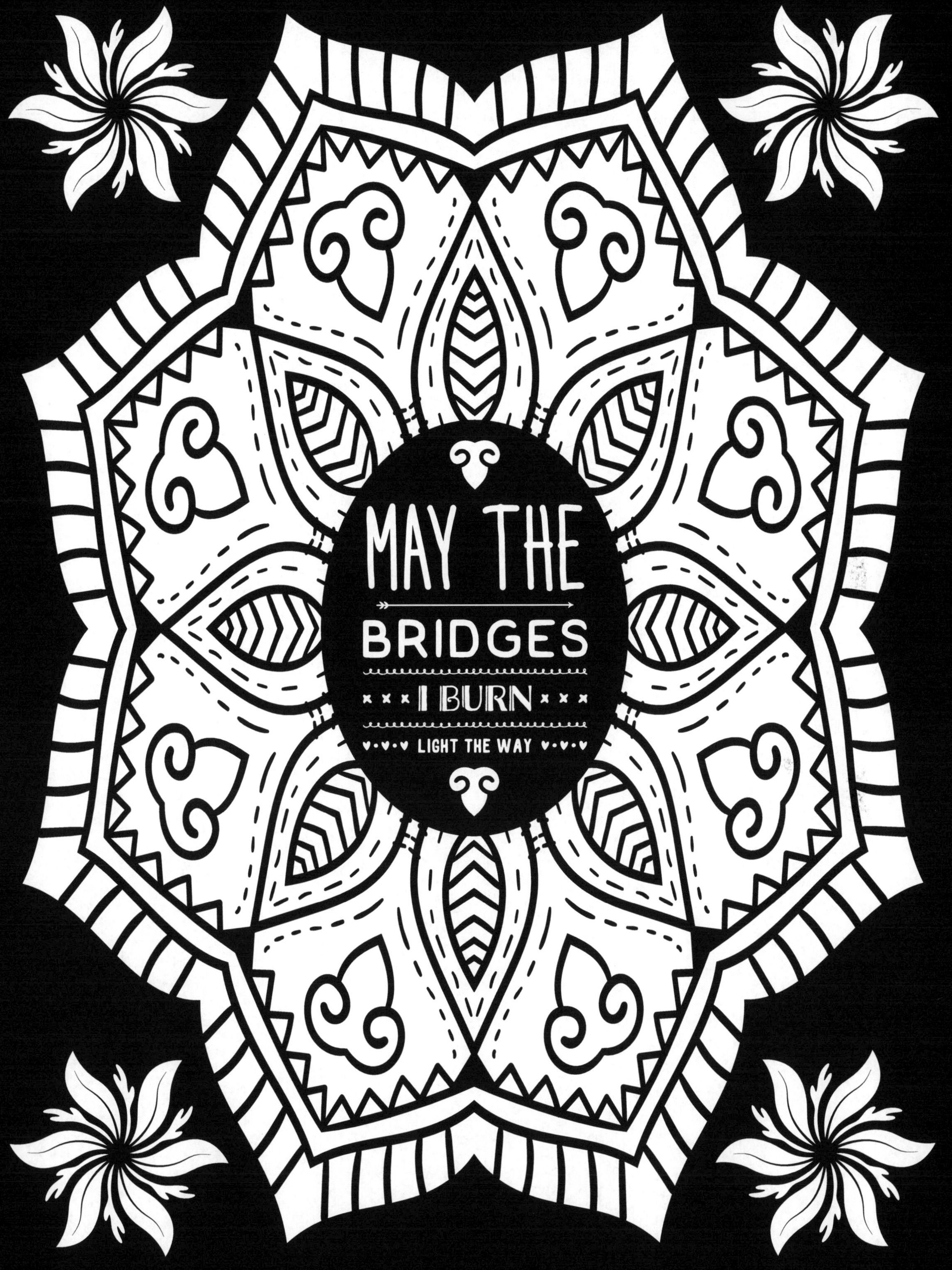
MAY THE
BRIDGES
I BURN
LIGHT THE WAY

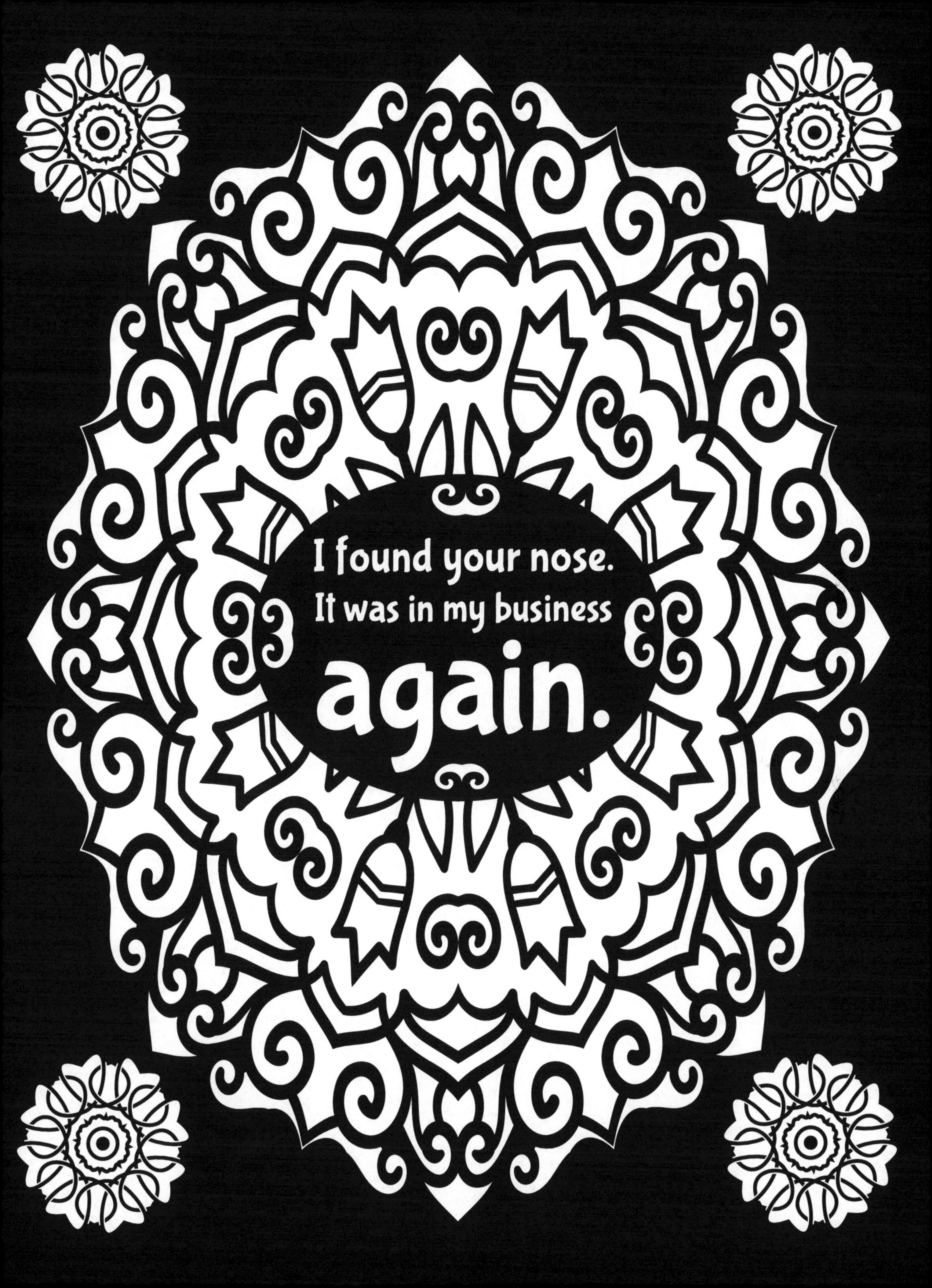
I found your nose.
It was in my business
again.

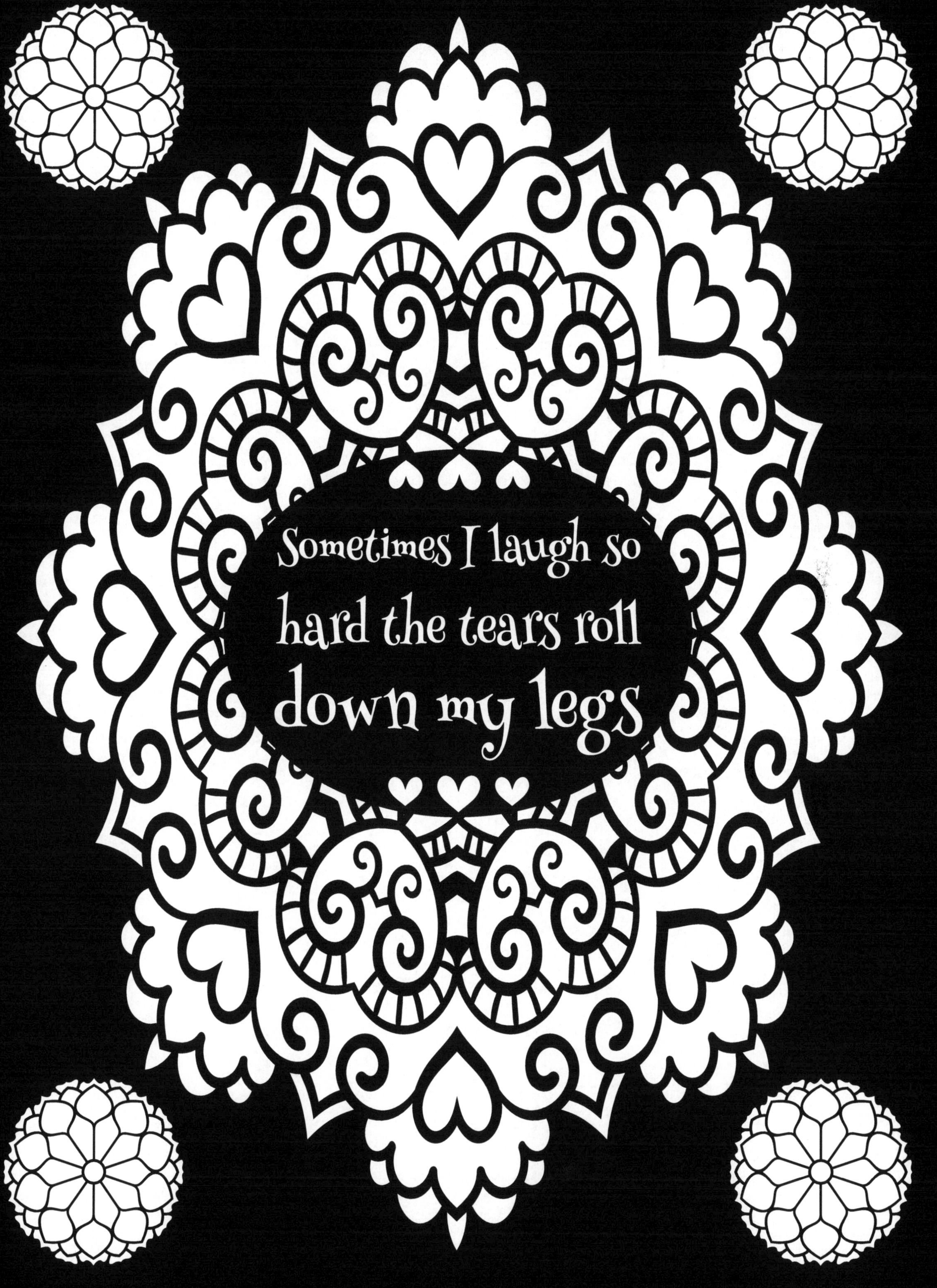
Sometimes I laugh so
hard the tears roll
down my legs

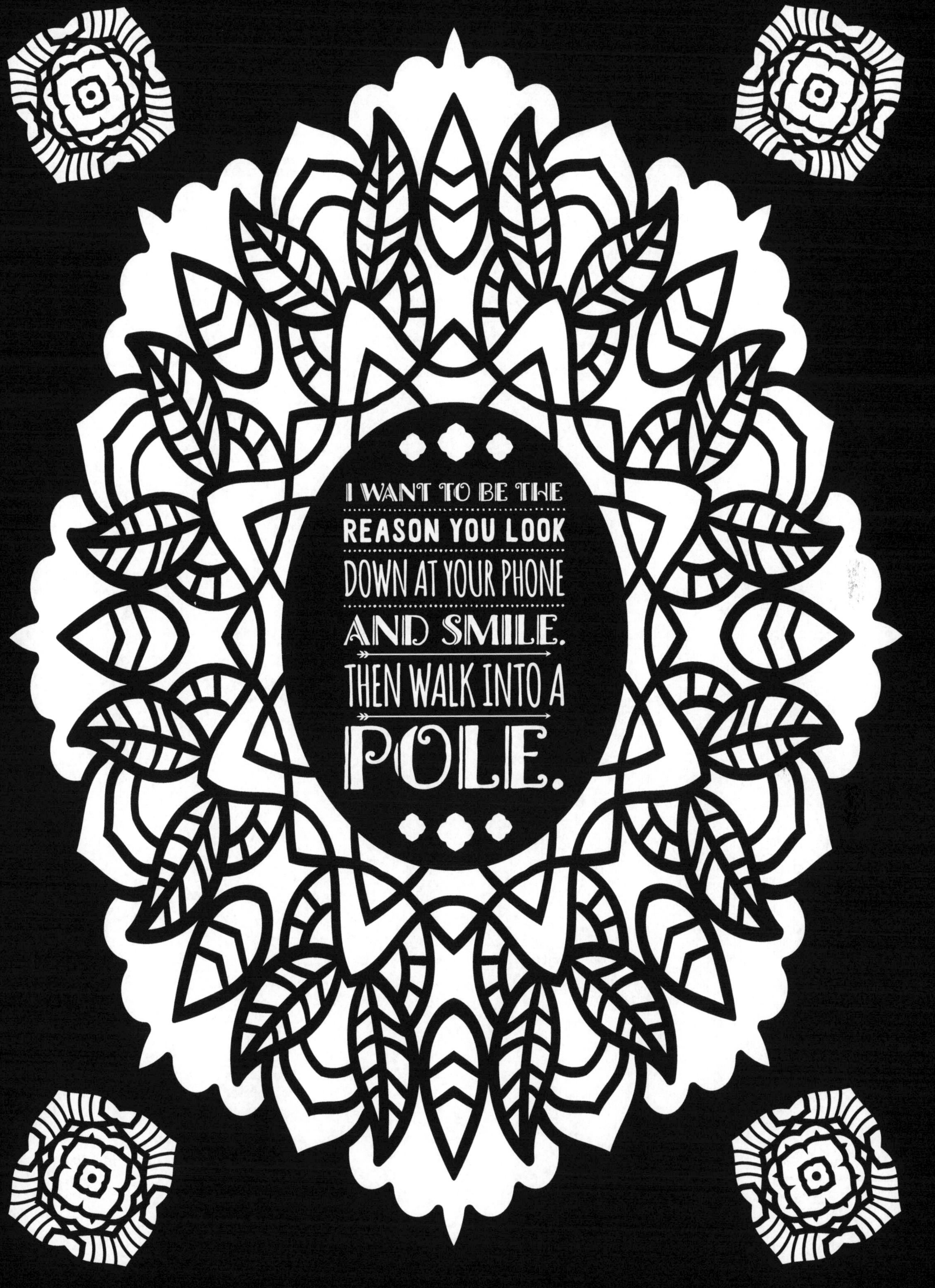
I WANT TO BE THE
REASON YOU LOOK
DOWN AT YOUR PHONE
AND SMILE.
THEN WALK INTO A
POLE.

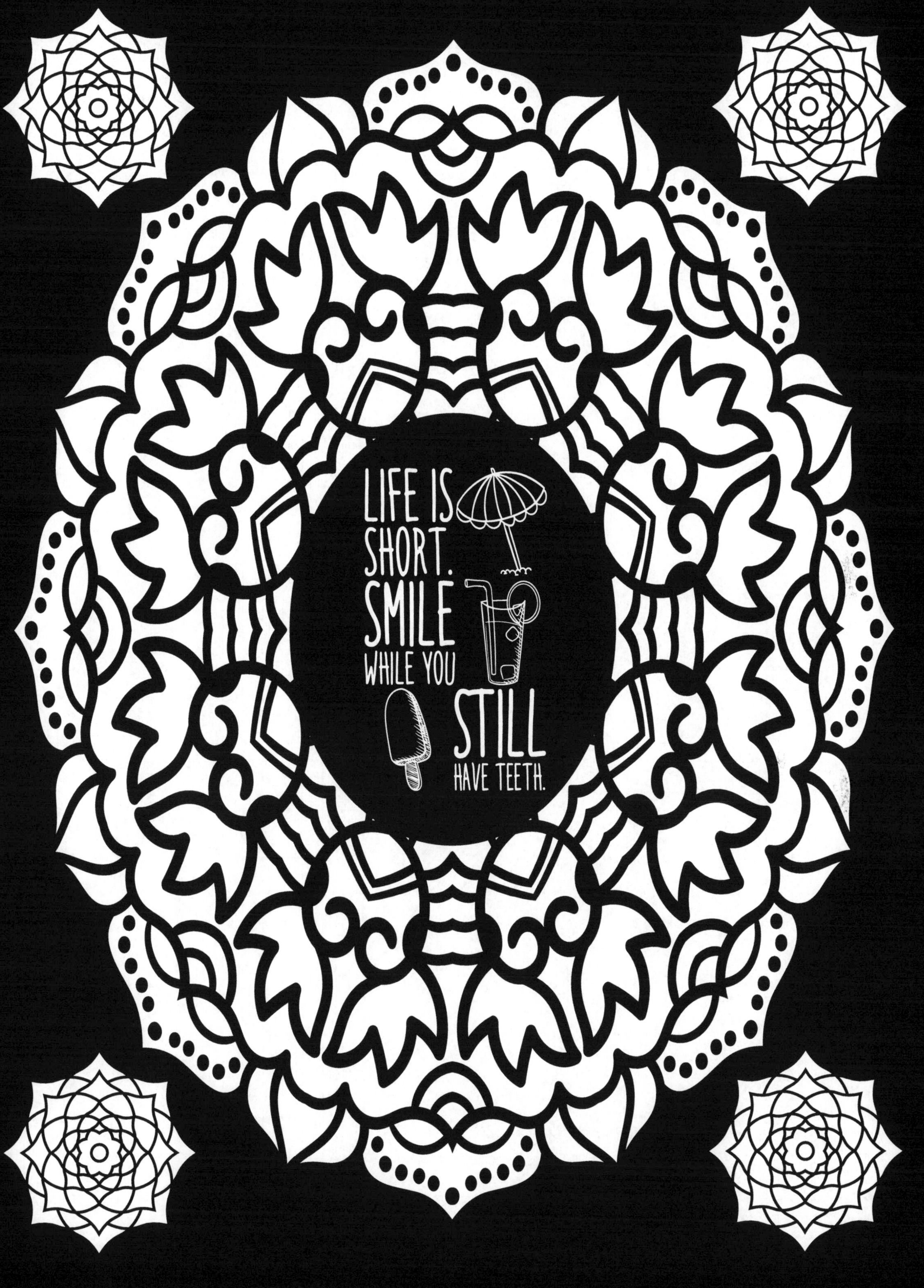
LIFE IS
SHORT.
SMILE
WHILE YOU
STILL
HAVE TEETH.

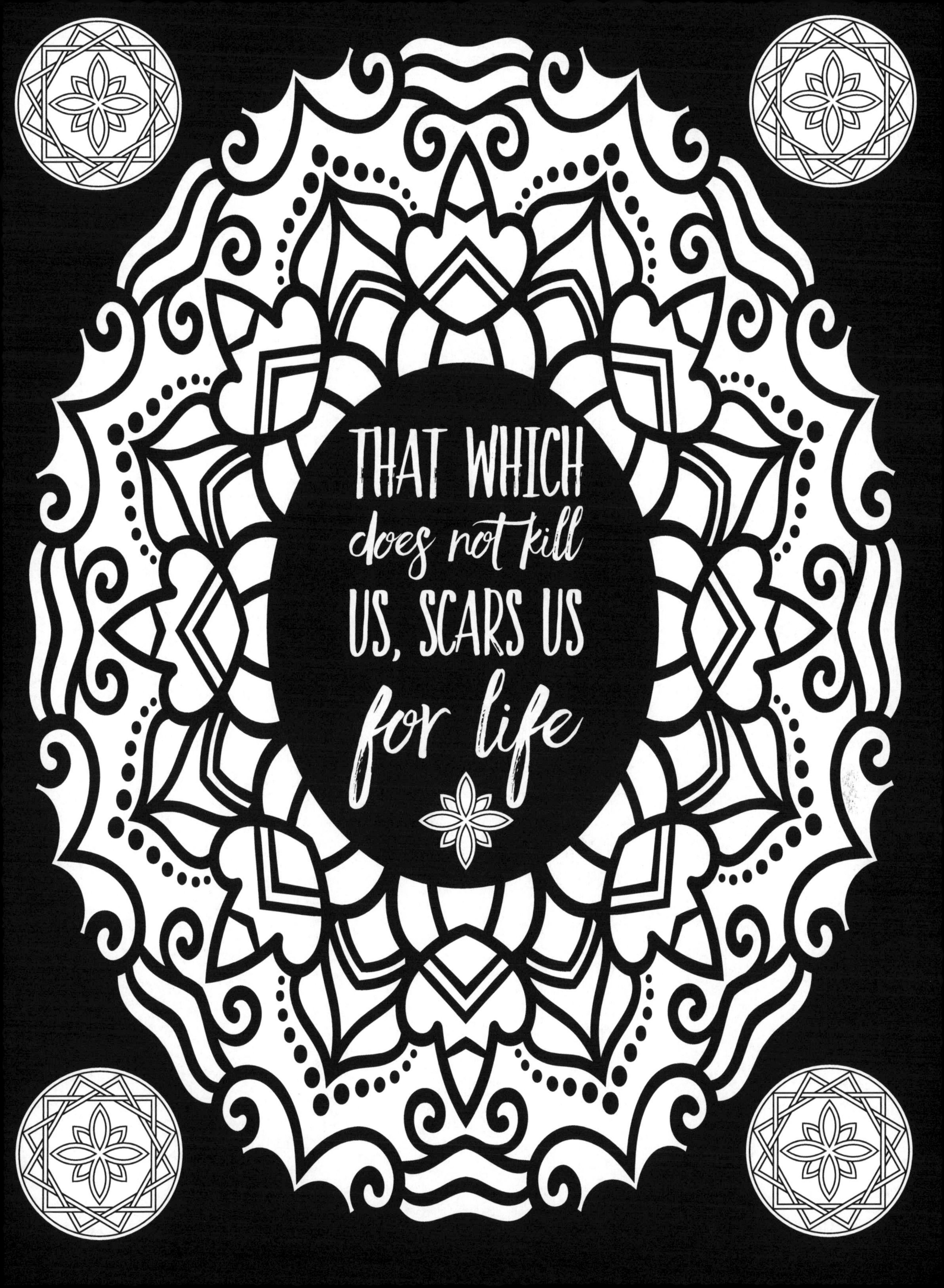
THAT WHICH
does not kill
US, SCARS US
for life

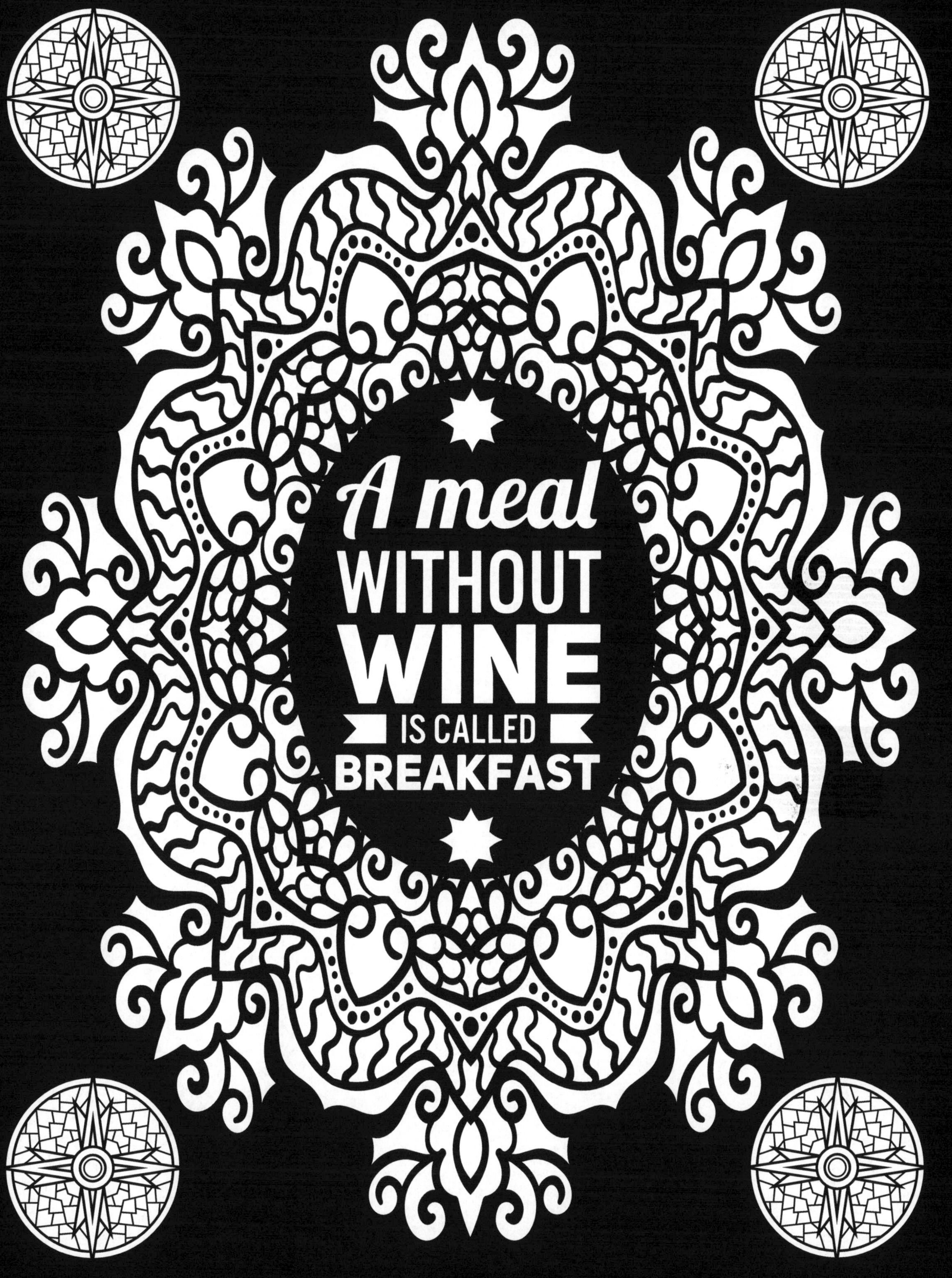
A meal
WITHOUT
WINE
IS CALLED
BREAKFAST

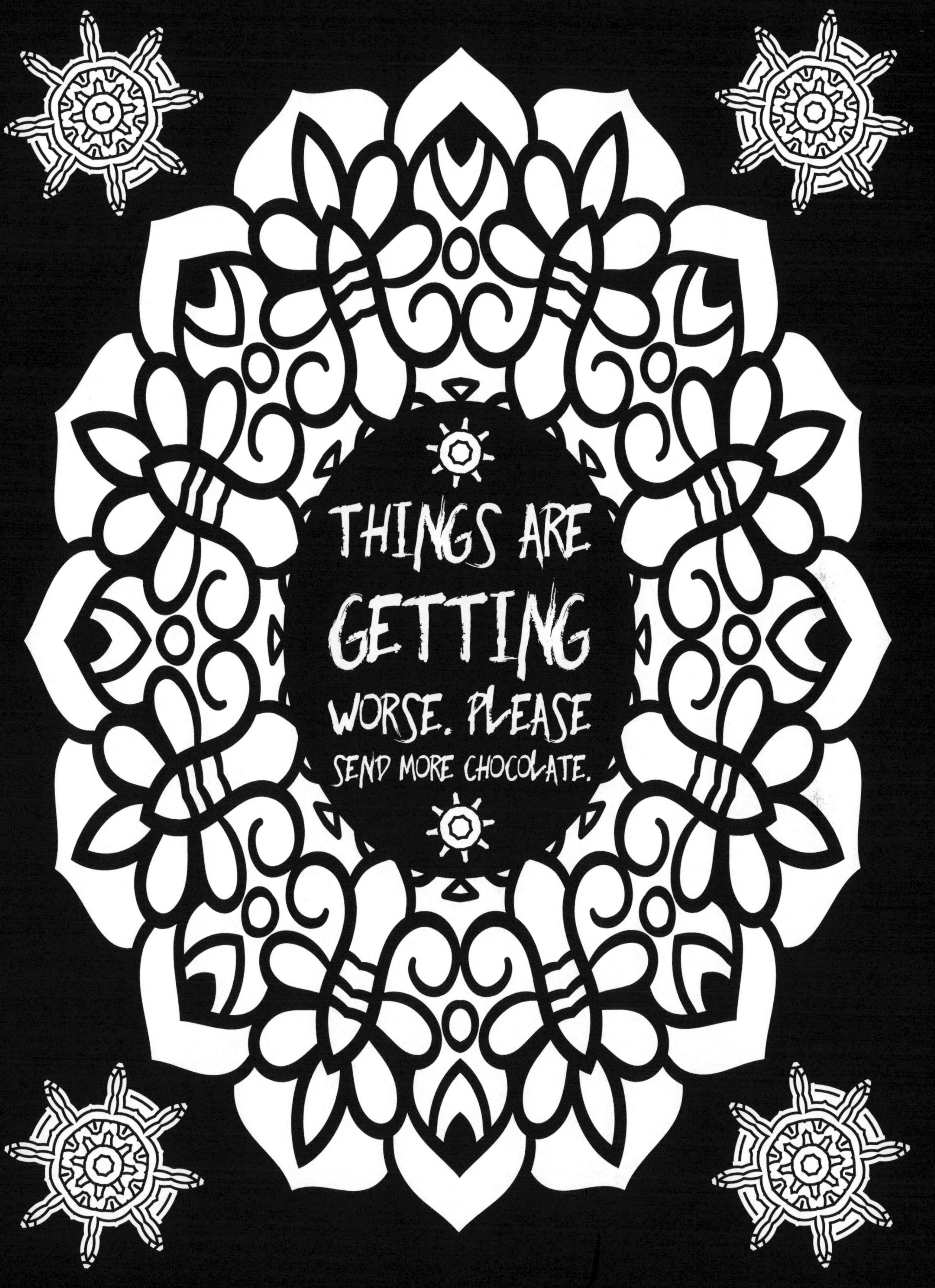
THINGS ARE
GETTING
WORSE. PLEASE
SEND MORE CHOCOLATE.

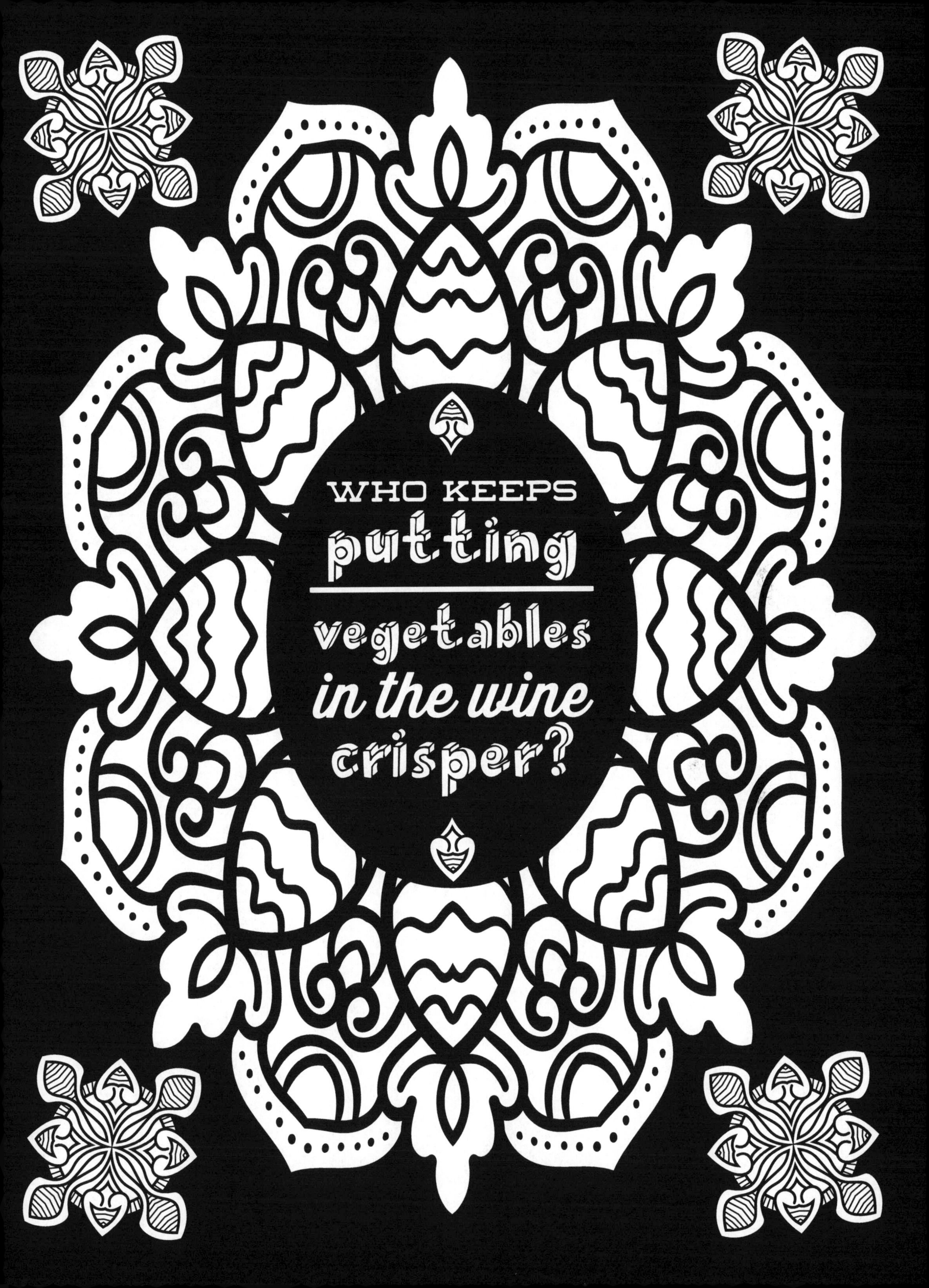
WHO KEEPS
putting
vegetables
in the wine
crisper?

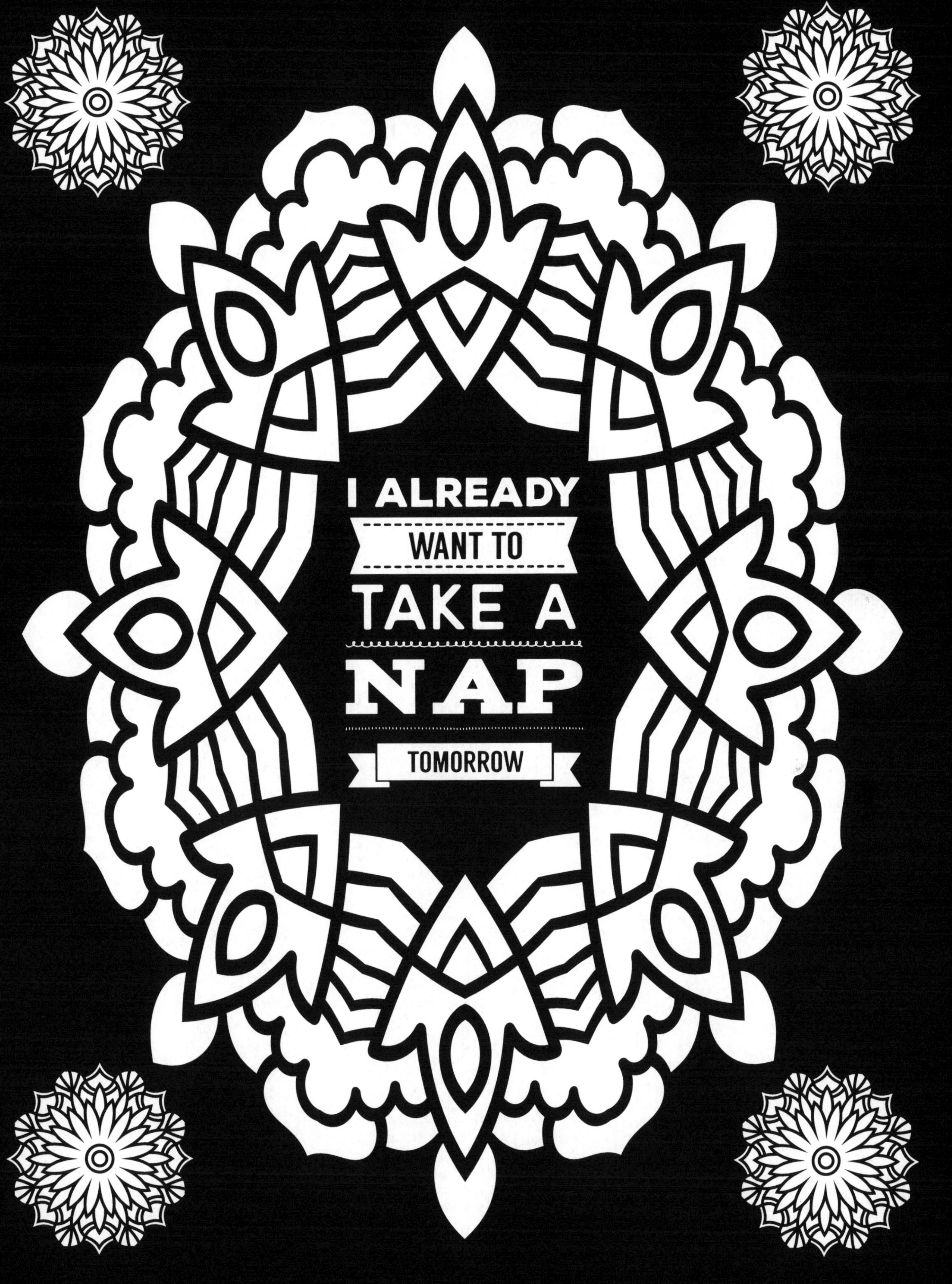
I ALREADY
WANT TO
TAKE A
NAP
TOMORROW

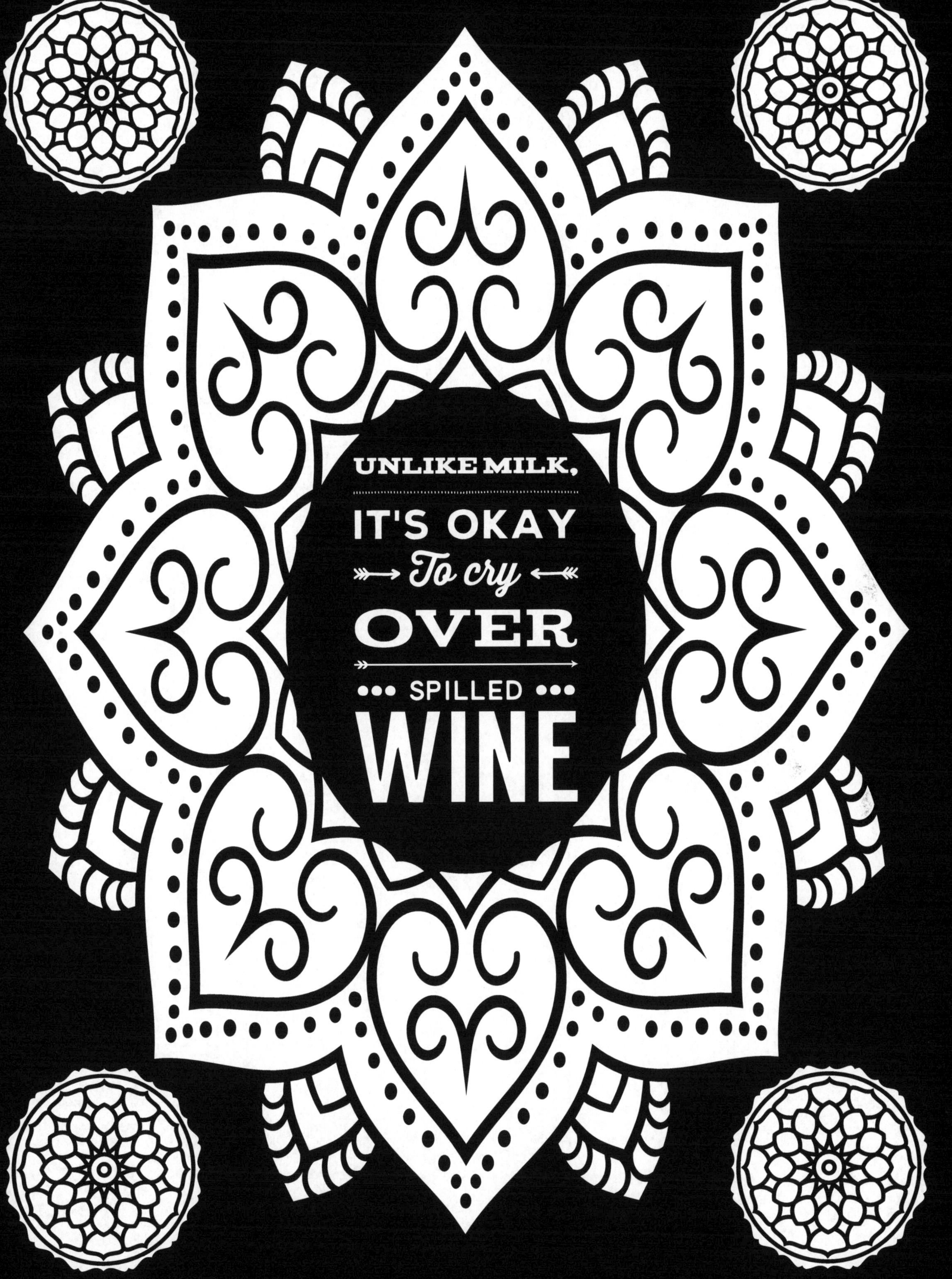
UNLIKE MILK,
IT'S OKAY
To cry
OVER
SPILLED
WINE

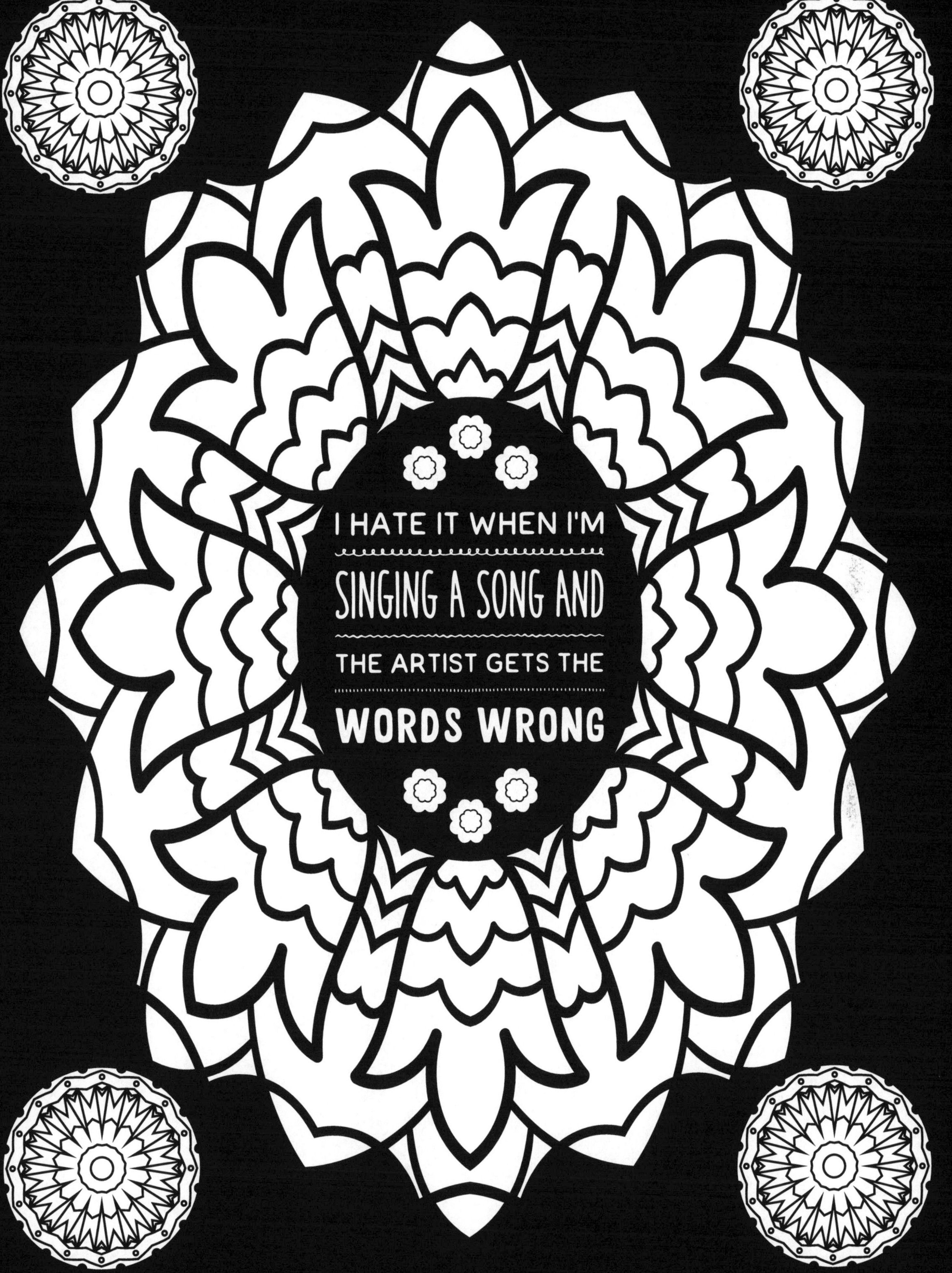
I HATE IT WHEN I'M
SINGING A SONG AND
THE ARTIST GETS THE
WORDS WRONG

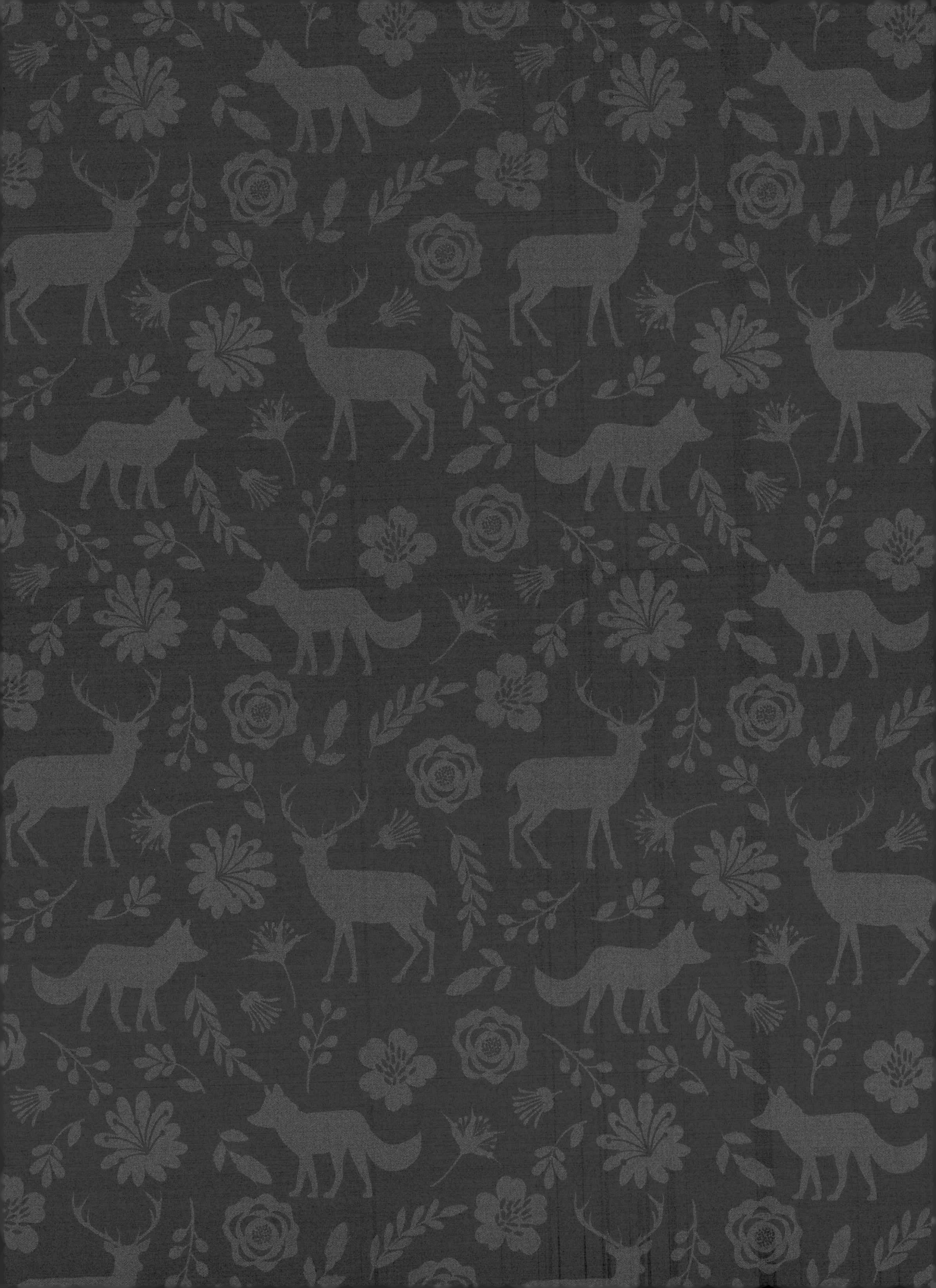

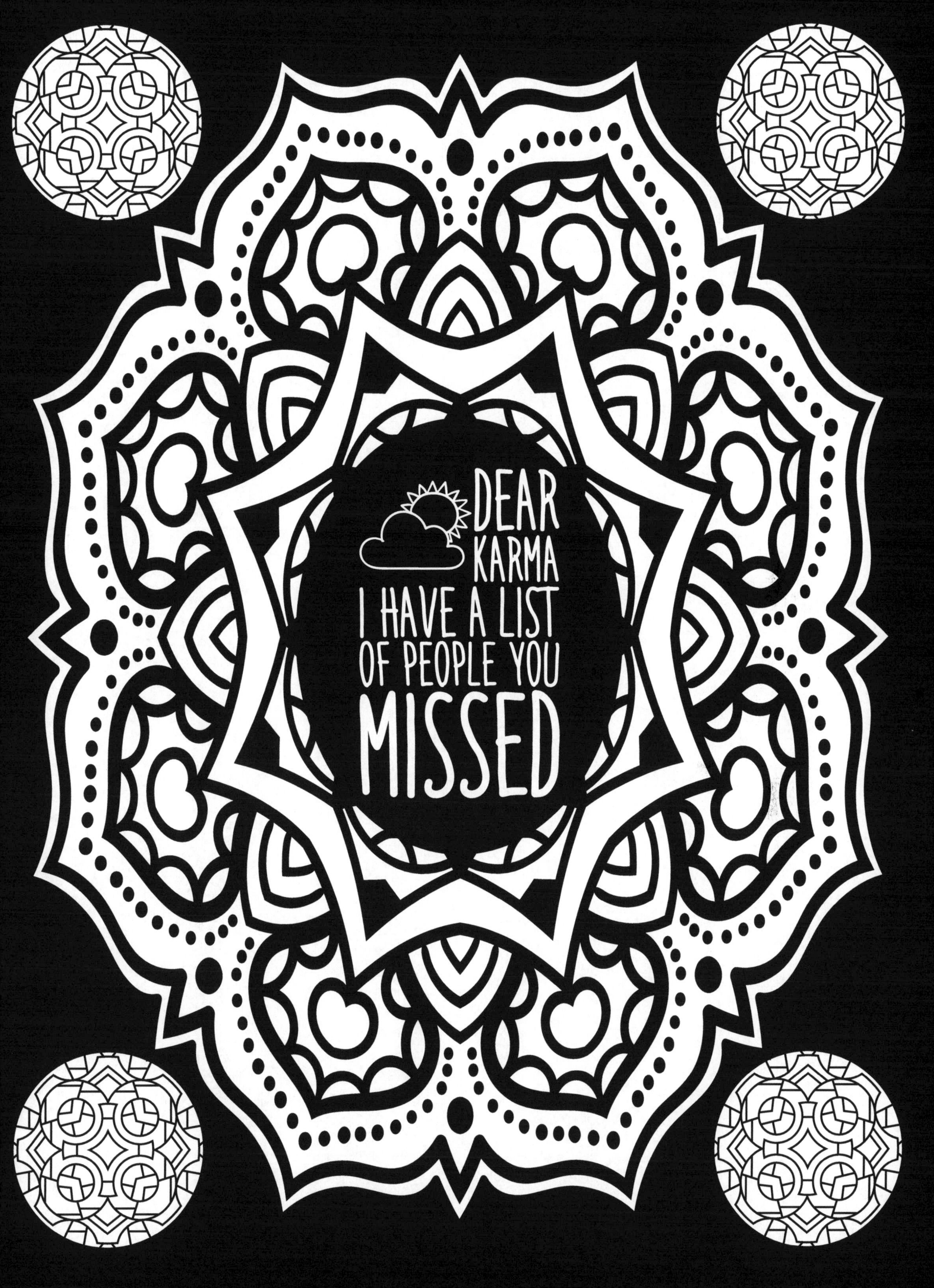
DEAR
KARMA
I HAVE A LIST
OF PEOPLE YOU
MISSED

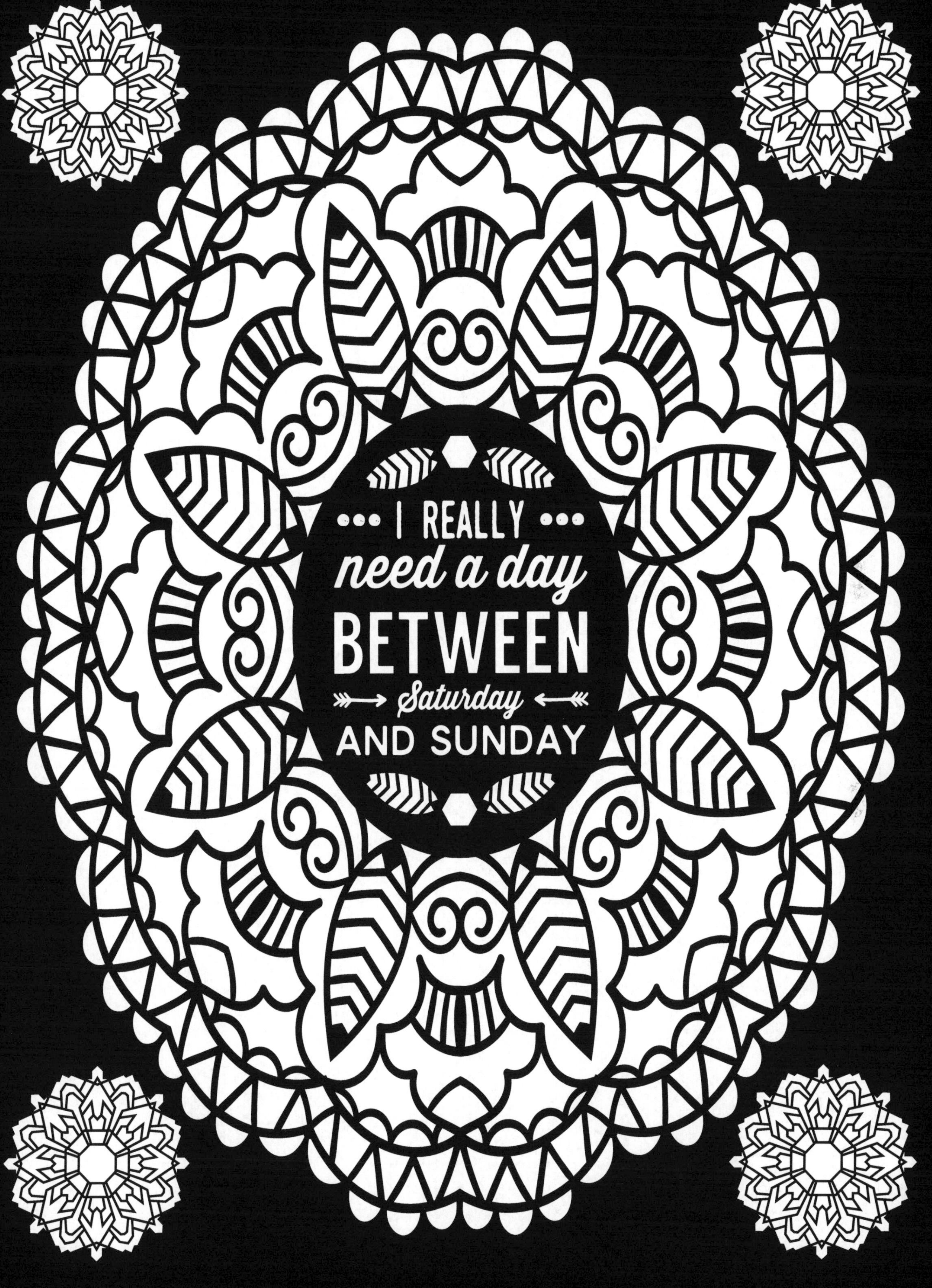
I REALLY
need a day
BETWEEN
Saturday
AND SUNDAY

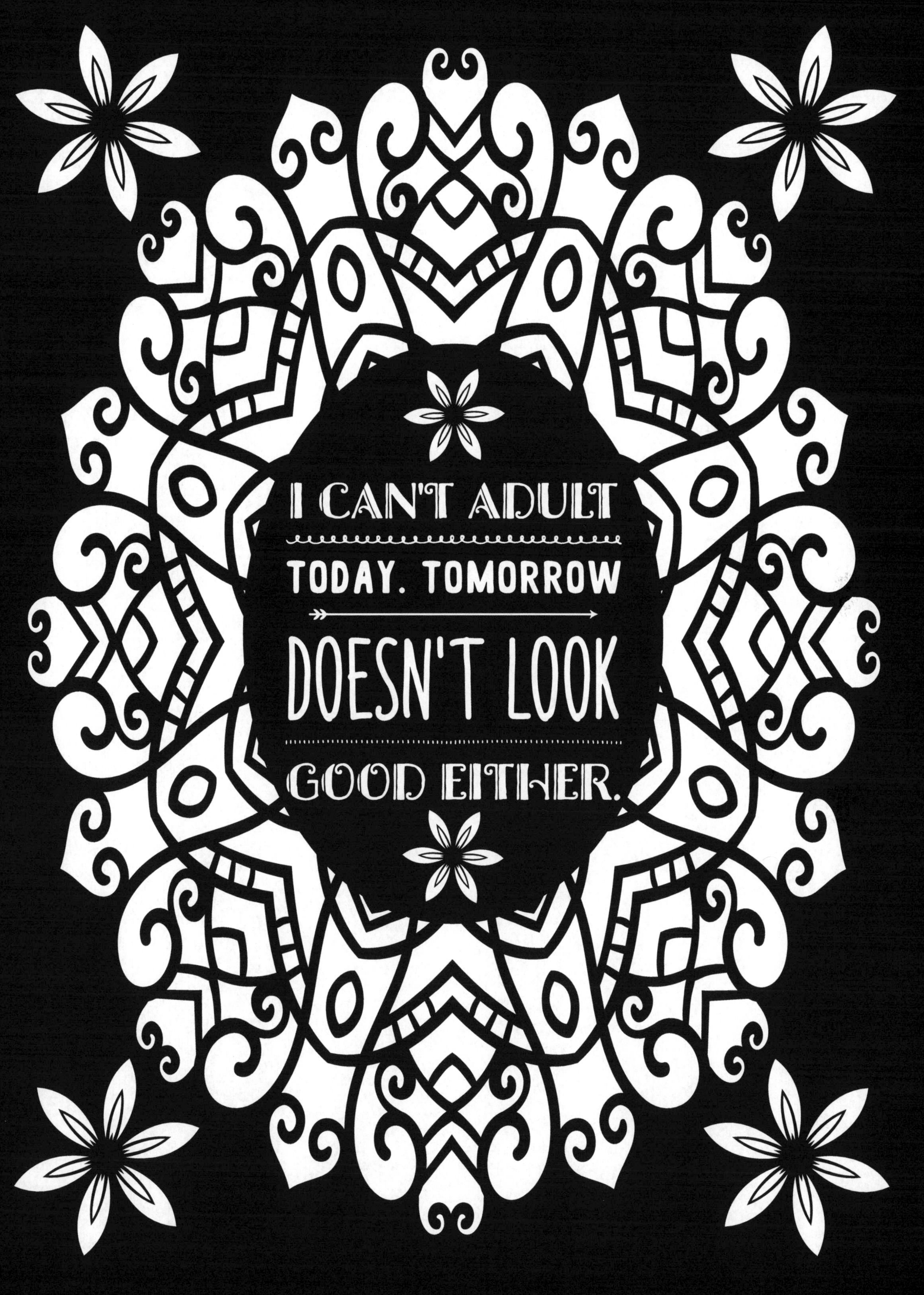
I CAN'T ADULT
TODAY. TOMORROW
DOESN'T LOOK
GOOD EITHER.

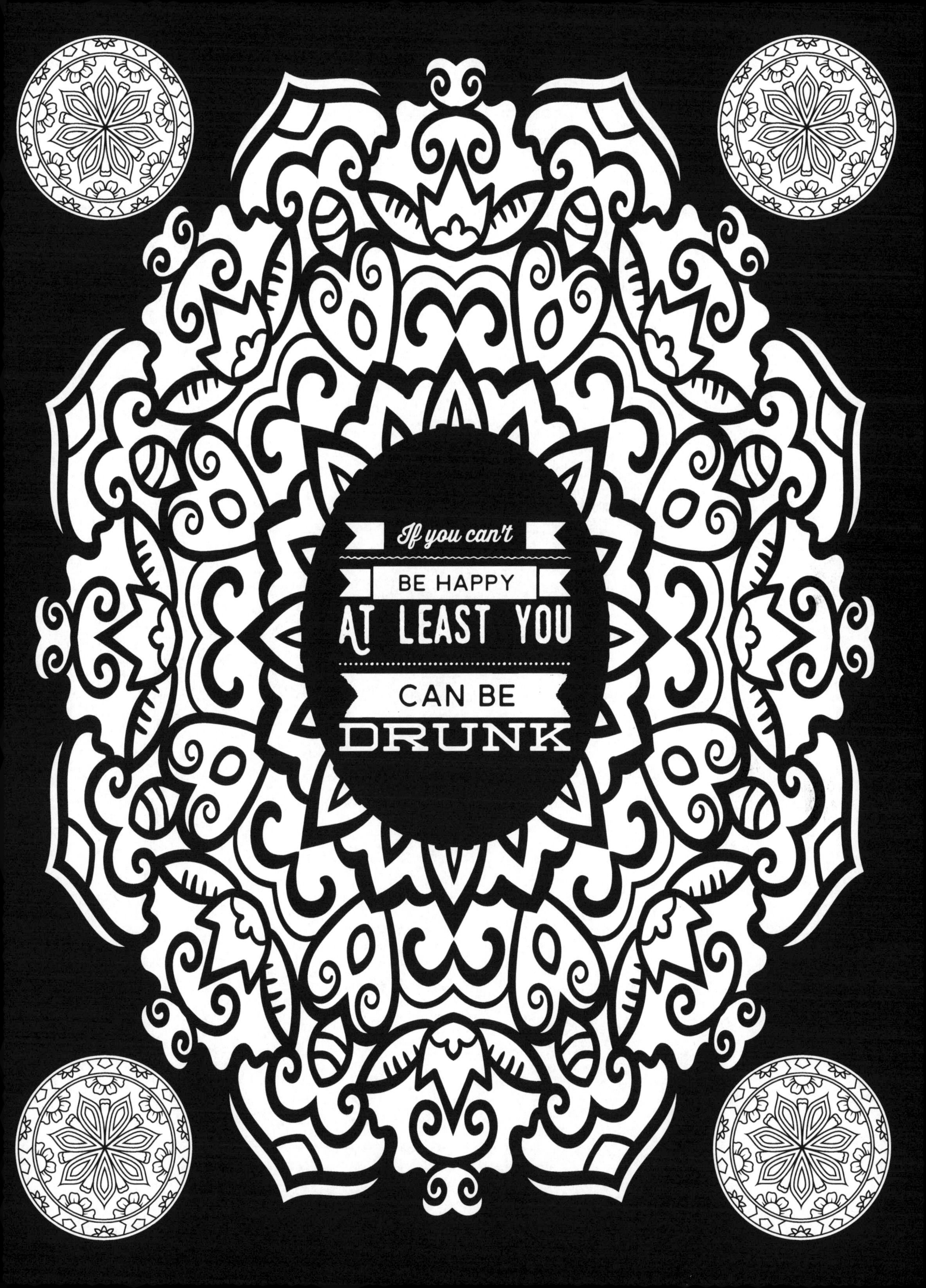
If you can't
BE HAPPY
AT LEAST YOU
CAN BE
DRUNK

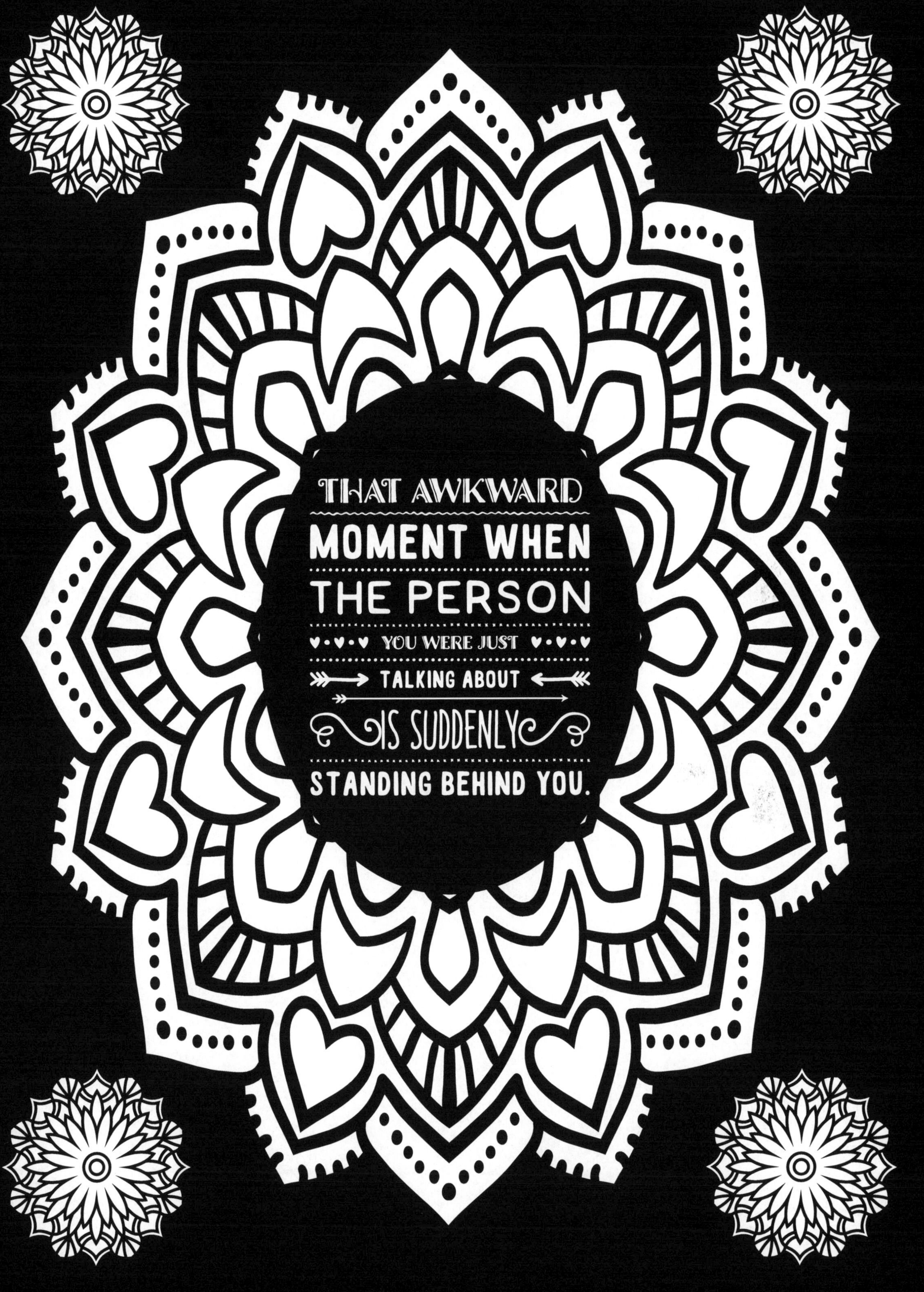
THAT AWKWARD
MOMENT WHEN
THE PERSON
YOU WERE JUST
TALKING ABOUT
IS SUDDENLY
STANDING BEHIND YOU.

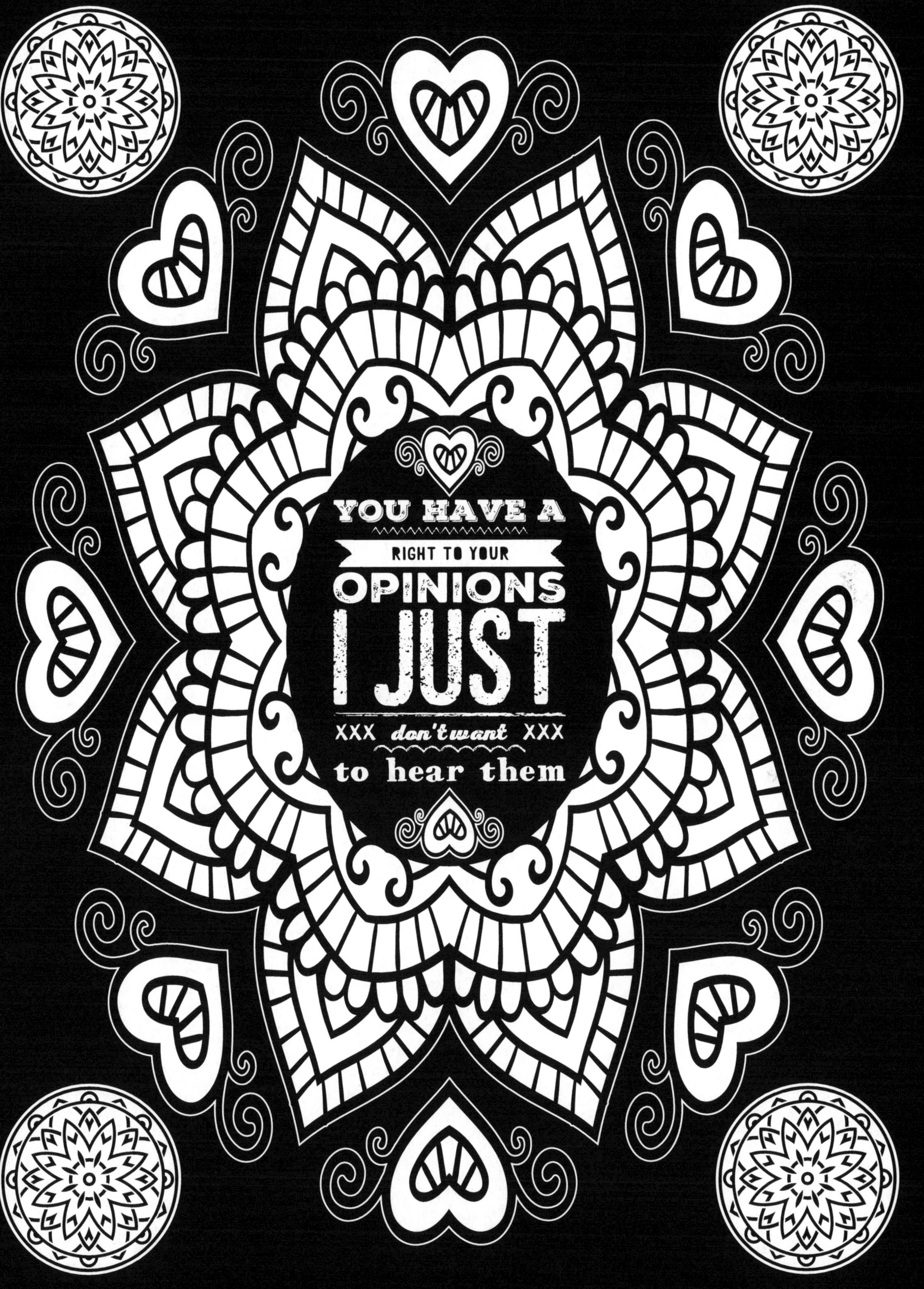
YOU HAVE A
RIGHT TO YOUR
OPINIONS
I JUST
XXX don't want XXX
to hear them

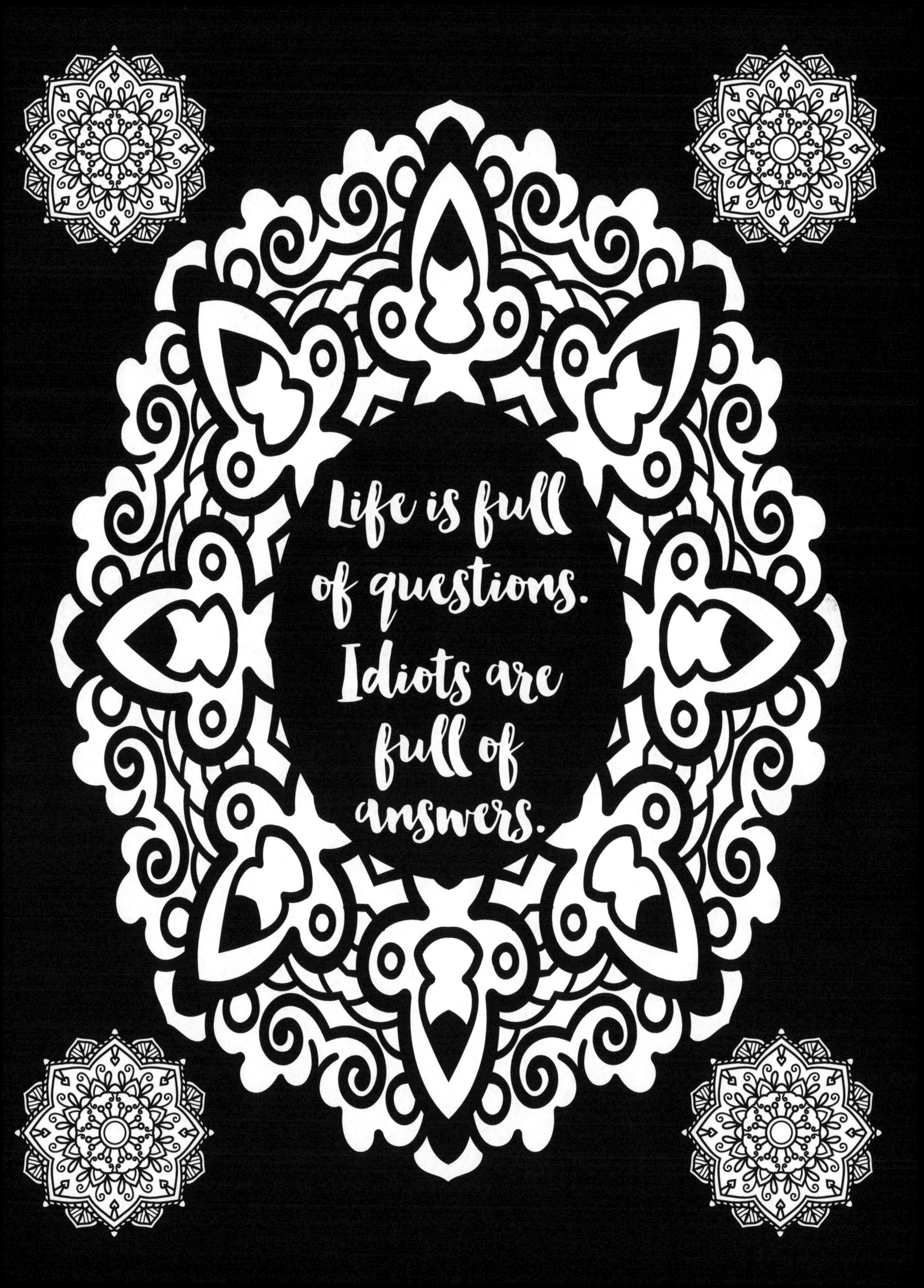
Life is full
of questions.
Idiots are
full of
answers.

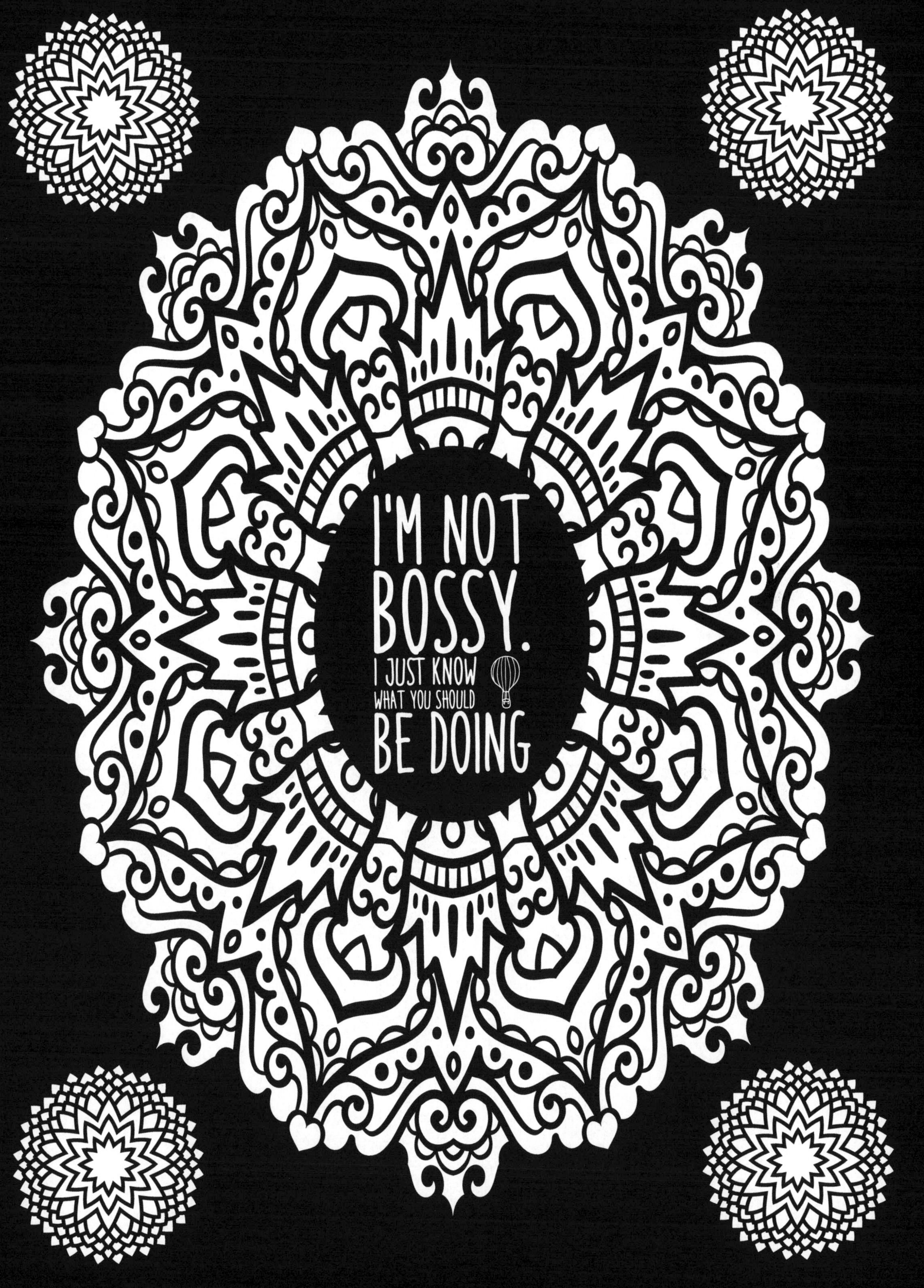
I'M NOT
BOSSY.
I JUST KNOW
WHAT YOU SHOULD
BE DOING

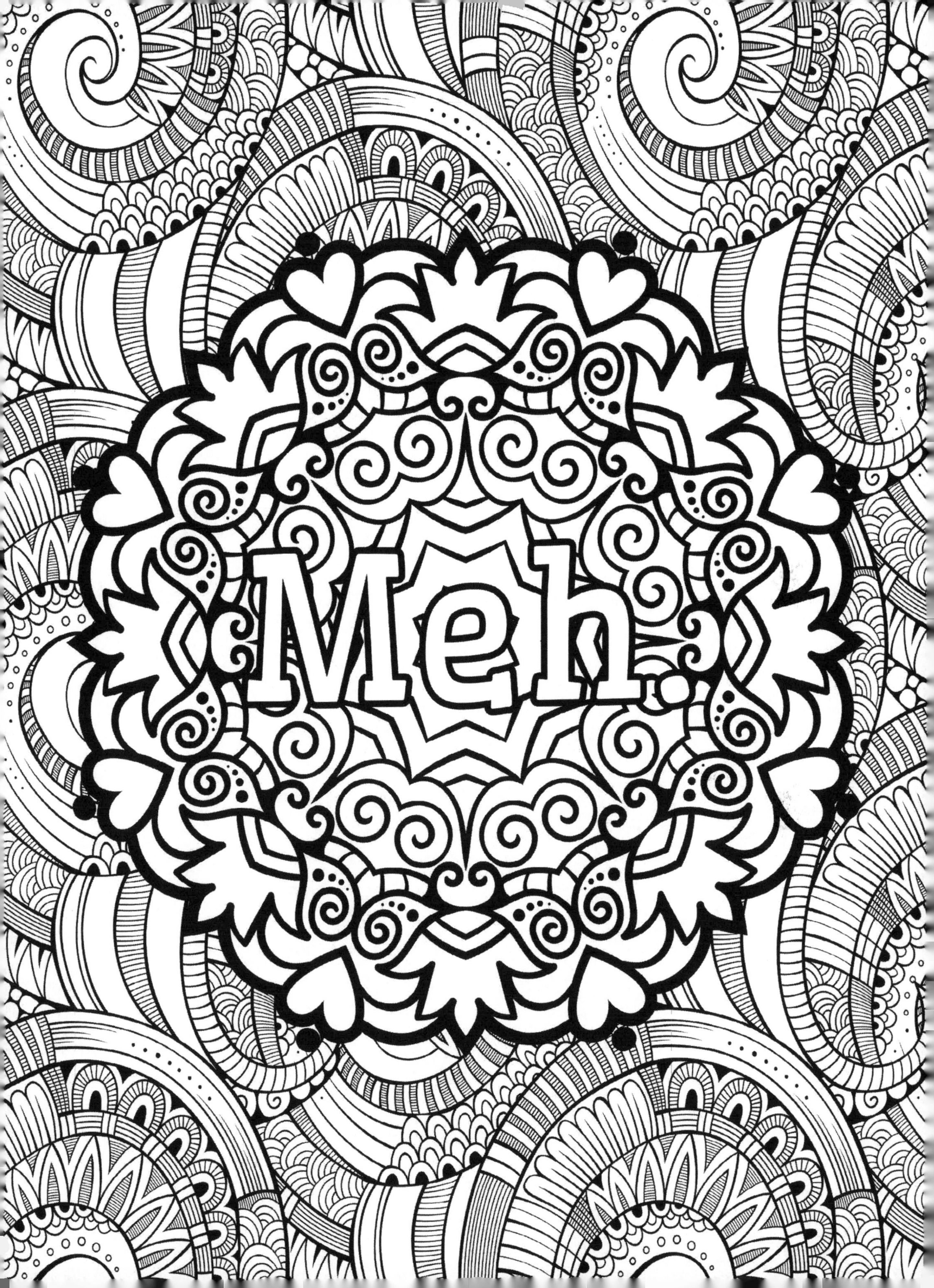
Meh.

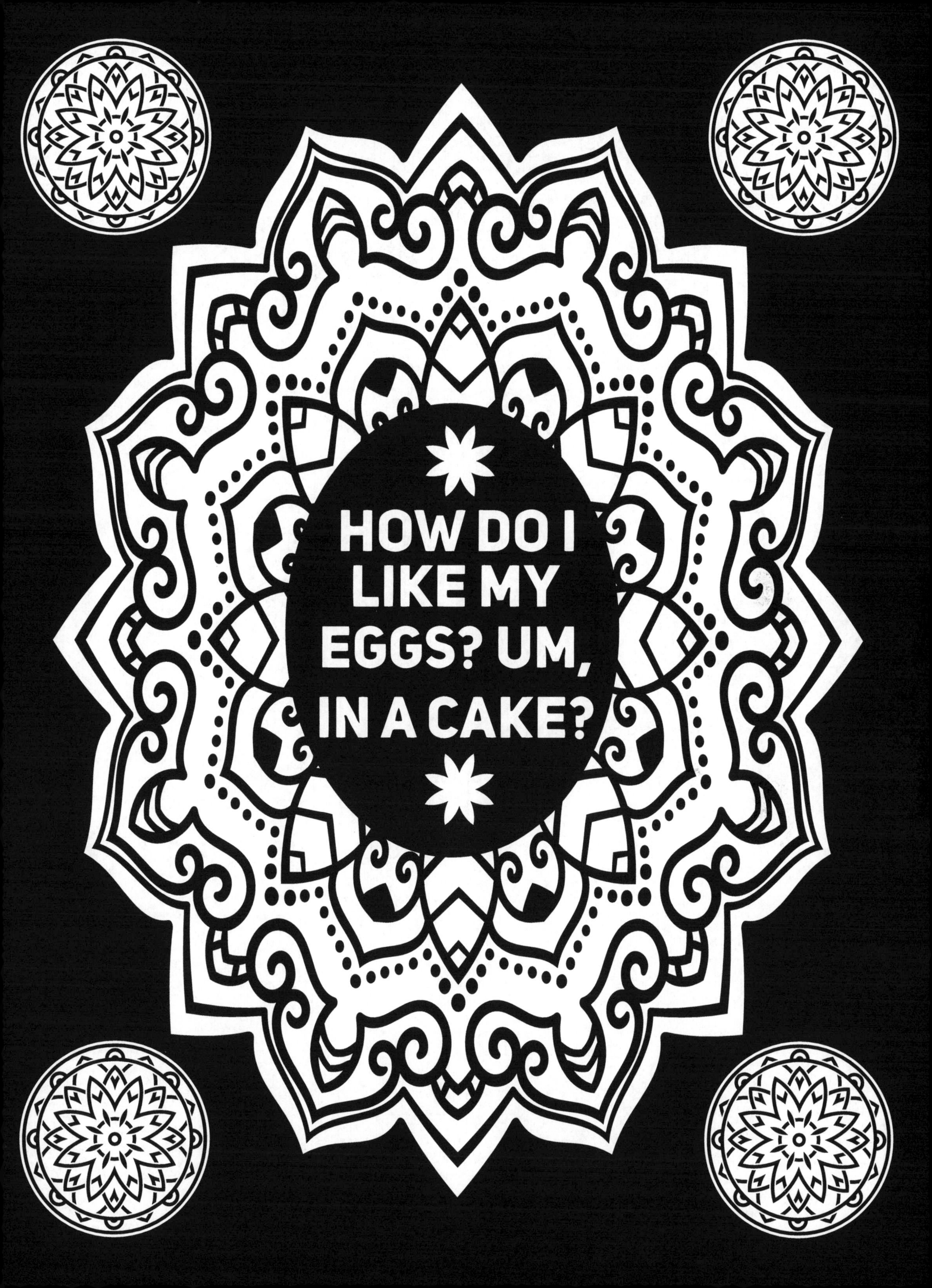
HOW DO I LIKE MY EGGS? UM, IN A CAKE?

BE SURE TO FOLLOW US ON SOCIAL MEDIA FOR THE LATEST NEWS, SNEAK PEEKS, & GIVEAWAYS

@PapeterieBleu

Papeterie Bleu

@PapeterieBleu

ADD YOURSELF TO OUR MONTHLY NEWSLETTER FOR FREE DIGITAL DOWNLOADS AND DISCOUNT CODES

www.papeteriebleu.com/newsletter

CHECK OUT OUR OTHER BOOKS!

www.papeteriebleu.com

    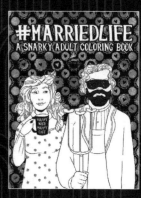

    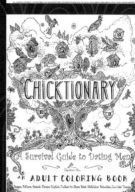

CHECK OUT OUR OTHER BOOKS!

www.papeteriebleu.com

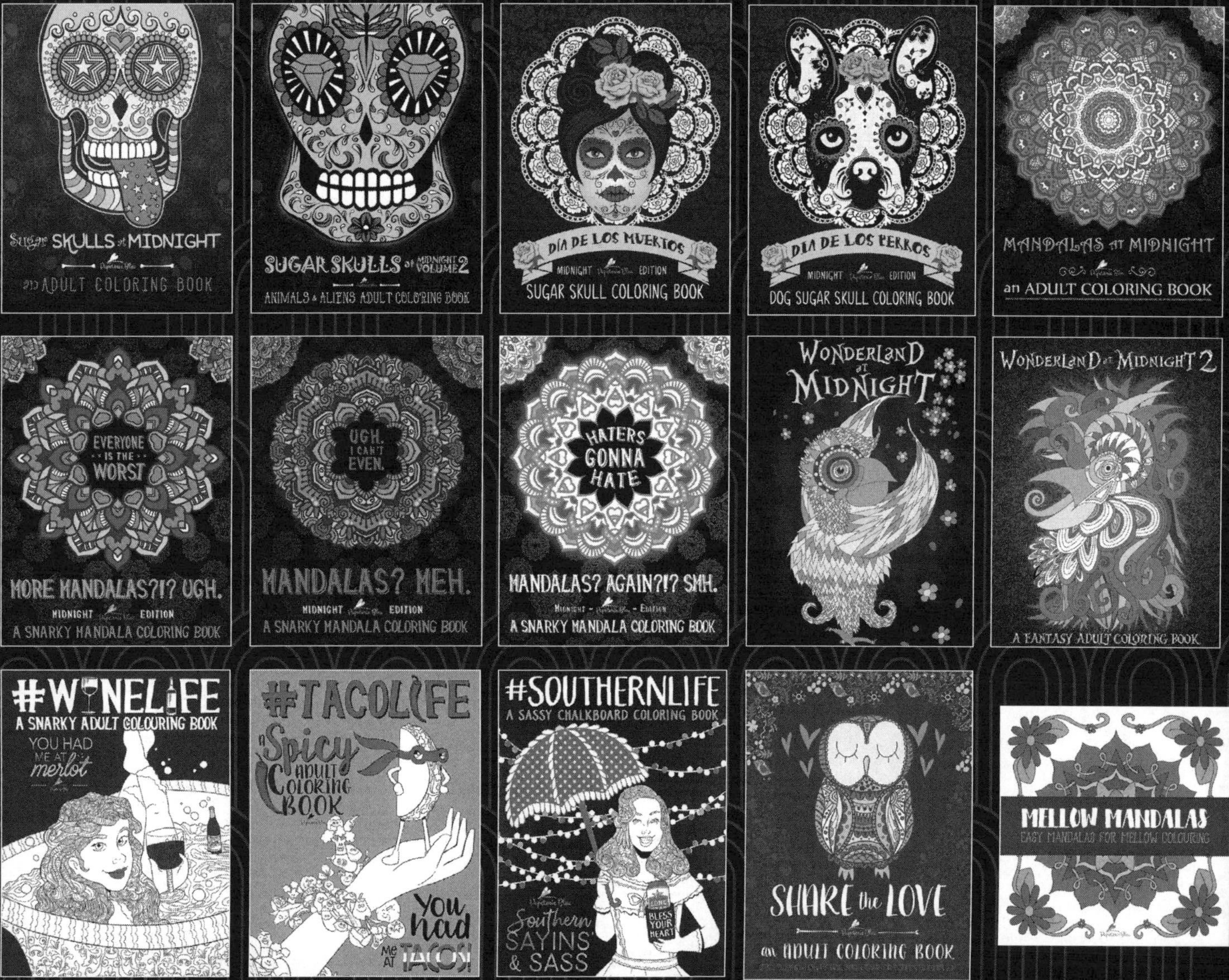
SUGAR SKULLS AT MIDNIGHT
AN ADULT COLORING BOOK
SUGAR SKULLS AT MIDNIGHT VOLUME 2
ANIMALS & ALIENS ADULT COLORING BOOK
DÍA DE LOS MUERTOS
MIDNIGHT EDITION
SUGAR SKULL COLORING BOOK
DÍA DE LOS PERROS
MIDNIGHT EDITION
DOG SUGAR SKULL COLORING BOOK
MANDALAS AT MIDNIGHT
an ADULT COLORING BOOK
EVERYONE IS THE WORST
MORE MANDALAS?!? UGH.
MIDNIGHT EDITION
A SNARKY MANDALA COLORING BOOK
UGH. I CAN'T EVEN.
MANDALAS? MEH.
MIDNIGHT EDITION
A SNARKY MANDALA COLORING BOOK
HATERS GONNA HATE
MANDALAS? AGAIN?!? SMH.
MIDNIGHT EDITION
A SNARKY MANDALA COLORING BOOK
WONDERLAND AT MIDNIGHT
WONDERLAND AT MIDNIGHT 2
A FANTASY ADULT COLORING BOOK
#WINELIFE
A SNARKY ADULT COLOURING BOOK
YOU HAD ME AT merlot
#TACOLIFE
a Spicy ADULT COLORING BOOK
You had me at TACOS!
#SOUTHERNLIFE
A SASSY CHALKBOARD COLORING BOOK
BLESS YOUR HEART
Southern SAYINS' & SASS
SHARE the LOVE
an ADULT COLORING BOOK
MELLOW MANDALAS
EASY MANDALAS FOR MELLOW COLOURING

CHECK OUT OUR OTHER BOOKS!

www.papeteriebleu.com

2017 weekly PLANNER
2017 weekly PLANNER
2017 weekly PLANNER
papeterie bleu
2017
weekly planner
MERRY CHRISTMAS
Word SEARCH
100 WORD SEARCH PUZZLES
VOLUME 1
Word SEARCH
100 WORD SEARCH PUZZLES
VOLUME 2
Word SEARCH
100 WORD SEARCH PUZZLES
VOLUME 3
SCRIBBLES DOODLES
STRESS RELIEVING DOODLE DESIGNS
FOLKLORIQUE
A FOLK ART COLORING BOOK
ADULT COLORING BOOK
ARTS DÉCORATIFS
ART DECO COLORING PATTERNS
PAPETERIE BLEU
浮世絵
UKIYO-E
JAPANESE WOODBLOCK COLORING BOOK
I RUN ON coffee SARCASM AND lipstick
A #SNARKY ADULT COLOURING BOOK
some people need a HIGH FIVE in the FACE with a CHAIR
A #SNARKY ADULT COLOURING BOOK
Champagne is my spirit animal
A #SNARKY ADULT COLOURING BOOK

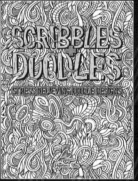

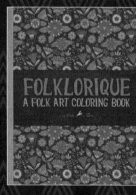

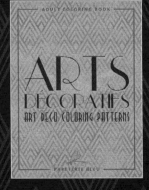

Made in the USA
Middletown, DE
21 December 2021